# CASALGUIDI STYLE
## LINEN EMBROIDERY

# Casalguidi Style
# LINEN EMBROIDERY

*Effie Mitrofanis*

Kangaroo Press

*Dedicated to the memory of my parents*
*Peter and Maria Cooley*

## Acknowledgments

My thanks to:
- My family for their support, especially my daughter and son-in-law Maria and Paul Galvin for their help with the props on page 20.
- My editor Anne Savage for her advice and skills in bringing this book together.
- DMC Needlecraft Pty Limited for supplying Zweigart fabrics and DMC threads for stitch samples and projects.
- Lee Sincic, photographer extraordinaire.
- Stadia Handcrafts for Permin linen fabrics and Mill Hill beads.
- Down Under Australia Pty Limited for threads by Caron, Needle Necessities and Rainbow.
- Minnamurra Threads for threads used in samples and projects.
- Orestis Saducas for translating from Italian to English Paolo Peri's article and material from *Il Ricamo di Casalguidi*, and for permission to reproduce his early twentieth century embroidered bedcover.
- The Embroiderers' Guild NSW Inc., Concord West, New South Wales, for permission to reproduce reticella embroidery and a seventeenth century sampler from the Guild collection, and permission to reproduce Roma Field's Casalguidi bag from *A Lifetime of Embroidery* by Roma Field, a limited edition published in 1980 by David Ell Press, Sydney.
- Wellington Embroiderers' Guild Inc., Wellington, New Zealand, for permission to reproduce their Casalguidi sachet.
- The Victorian Embroiderers' Guild, Malvern, Victoria, for permission to reproduce their Casalguidi lion bag.
- Valerie Carson, Textile Conservator of Eastbourne, New Zealand, for permission to reproduce her Casalguidi lion bag.
- Irene Mitrofanis, my sister-in-law, for lending me her family treasures.
- In New Zealand—Julie Jackson for finding the antique bag and letting me have it, Helen Marshall and Avis Swann for contributions of information and photos.
- My friend Heather Joynes and workshop participants Anne Atkin, Jeanette Blunsden, Pamela Gordon, Lynne Leighton and Beryl Rutter for permission to use their work and Doris Waltho for the use of her Venetian bead necklace.

*Photography—Lee Sincic*
*Styling and design—Effie Mitrofanis*

FRONTISPIECE *One of the most popular designs, characteristic of Casalguidi embroidery, is two hexagons of padded raised stem band with Venetian rosettes and overcasting on a background of modified four-sided stitch and embellished with bobbles. Italian, early twentieth century. Collection of the author.*

COVER *Gryphon bag by Effie Mitrofanis. Mythical animals such as the gryphon and the dragon were often the source of embroidery designs. The gryphon is worked on a background of four-sided stitch with surface stitches of buttonhole stitch space filler, bullions, wrapping and overcasting worked in coton perle no. 8. The bag's shape and the elaborate tassels were inspired by a traditional Casalguidi bag. The tassels are a combination of buttonhole stitched bobbles on a quilt wadding foundation with buttonholed chained rings.*

*Reprinted in 1997*
*First published in 1996 by Kangaroo Press Pty Ltd*
*An imprint of Simon & Schuster Australia*
*20 Barcoo Street (PO Box 507) East Roseville 2069*
*Printed in Hong Kong through Colorcraft Ltd*

ISBN 0 86417 755 0

# CONTENTS

Casalguidi embroidery is a style of white-linen embroidery, named after a small village near Pistoia in Italy, which emerged in the late 1800s and flourished until World War I.

*The linen cupboard first appeared at the end of the fourteenth century as a piece of kitchen furniture, thus beginning the history of the trousseau which reached its highest point in nineteenth century Europe.*

# ᗉNTRODUCTION

My introduction to Casalguidi embroidery came in the early 1980s, when I saw several examples in books about white embroidery and stumpwork, techniques with which I was already familiar.

Although Casalguidi embroidery is mentioned in a few English books and magazines very little is written about it other than that it was worked in the late nineteenth century in the village of Casalguidi near Pistoia in Italy and was 'associated with nuns in convents'. Although examples appear in a few publications, the only detailed instructions in English that I am aware of are in the *Anchor Manual of Needlework* (first published 1958) in a chapter titled 'Various types of embroidery', in particular the section on Italian embroidery. The chapter opens with the words: 'It could be said that in every corner of Italy there is a different kind of embroidery.' It refers to the drawn-thread work of Sicily and Sardinia, the laces of Venice and Cantu, the tablecloths of Assisi, the ancient stitches deriving from antique lace. Orvieto, Siena, Parma are among the centres of embroidery mentioned, but there are many other types of embroidery throughout Italy, such as Palestrina, Perugino and Byzantine embroidery, which originated and developed in Ravenna where the Byzantine art of the churches and palaces offers an inexhaustible source of inspiration. The designs are, in fact, taken from the architecture of Ravenna and from the famous mosaics which decorate the Cathedral. Sorbello embroidery is named after the small Neapolitan village where it is worked. Other types mentioned are Deruta embroidery, after a small town in Umbria, Canusina from the town of Canossa, Parma from the province of Lombardy, Bricco, Arezzo and the beautiful Florentine or Italian quilting. The *Anchor Manual of Needlework* describes Casalguidi simply as 'a small place near Pistoia which gives its name to this type of embroidery'. It provides a photograph of a heavily embroidered table runner with a large tassel on each corner decorated with a mesh hood and bullion knots, and gives a method of working padded raised stem stitch and some of the traditional Casalguidi stitch motifs.

The technical instructions in this book have evolved from reading hundreds of reference books and from my own knowledge and experience, adapted and, I hope, simplified. I am grateful to all the embroiderers who have attended my workshops and classes in Australia and New Zealand whose questions and input have stretched me, refined the stitch instructions and enriched my awareness.

It wasn't until recently when I received an article from the Museo Davanzati di Firenze by Paolo Peri, published in Florence in 1986 and titled 'The Stitches of Casalguidi and the Art of Embroidery' that a larger, local historical picture became available. The information and detail in this article have enriched my awareness of the historical background and characteristics of the style. Without the language expertise of a family friend, Orestis Saducas, the article would have remained untranslated.

The antiques shown in the historical chapter (pages 11–12) and the articles in the photograph on the opposite page have been made available by the Embroiderers' Guild NSW, Embroiderers' Guild Victoria, the Wellington Embroiderers' Guild (New Zealand), from the private collections of Valerie Carson and the author, and from the family heirlooms of Irene Mitrofanis, Orestis Saducas and the author.

Valerie Carson, a textile conservator from New Zealand, found her 'lion bag' in an antique shop in Nelson, New Zealand, about ten years ago (see page 18). Interestingly, the owner said it had been in the shop for ten years before that and Valerie was the first person to show any interest in it. Valerie: 'I saw it, recognised it for what it was instantly and coveted it immediately.'

My own Casalguidi bag (see page 2) was acquired in Auckland, New Zealand, in 1995 when I visited there to give workshops. Julie Jackson of Auckland found the bag in an

*Historic centres of embroidery*

antique shop there and offered it to me when she attended the workshops so that more people would be able to appreciate its beauty. It had only arrived in Auckland two weeks before from a buyer's trip to an antique shop in Covent Garden, London. It was a very exciting experience for all those who attended the workshops to see and touch the exquisite beauty of the real thing and finally to look at the back of the embroidery, which revealed a modified four-sided stitch I hadn't seen before.

Casalguidi work encompasses many aspects of embroidery which are particularly interesting. First of all the technique itself, rich in texture and relief and resembling sculptured marble, an effect created by the padded raised embroidery on an open background and the rough texture of needlelace, buttonholed bars and raised stem band contrasted with the smoothness of bullion knots and overcast and wrapped scrolls. The surface embroidery is often described as being similar to stumpwork, the elaborate raised embroidery popular in England in the seventeenth century. The added opulence of Italian style bobbles, tassels, picots and button tassels gives Casalguidi embroidery its own unique and appealing style.

Casalguidi embroidery's interest lies also in its

place as a cottage industry in a century when cottage industries abounded. Of importance here is women's part in providing a primary or secondary income in times of famine and rural hardship. In fact, in Italy cottage industries are referred to as *industrie femminili* (women's industries) and *lavori femminili* (women's work).

The history of Casalguidi is followed by a glossary, the basic techniques and handy hints on embroidery techniques in general, the use of needles, and transferring a design to fabric.

The chapter on materials and equipment gives details of the vast range of colourful linens and threads now available to the embroiderer. I am grateful for all the information, Zweigart fabrics and DMC threads provided by DMC Needlecraft in Sydney.

The next chapter deals with a number of ways in which the background for the embroidery may be prepared with four-sided stitch and modified four-sided stitch, both a very distinctive part of the Casalguidi style. The different surface stitches used in Casalguidi embroidery and instructions for working them are outlined in the next section.

The section on embellishments covers two types of hems to finish off the embroidered article, insertion stitches to join the edges together, and the decorative additions of tassels, bobbles, buttons, loops, cords and picots.

The projects are divided into several categories, with diagrams, patterns, materials and full instructions given for four beautiful traditional motifs inspired by historical examples; an antique bag, pouches and purses; designs for cushions, bags and wall panels; table linen; household linen; scented sachets and pillows; brooches.

All the original projects, designed and made by the author, are inspired by the traditional stitches and techniques of Casalguidi embroidery but use contemporary coloured linens and threads, flowers and geometric motifs. Traditional characteristics of the style are retained while additions and modifications are adapted to contemporary materials and applications for monochromatic and colourful designs.

The gallery and some of the chapter opening pages show embroideries based on the Casalguidi style worked by workshop participants and the author. Some are quite experimental, being worked on painted canvas or dyed fabric.

Others are inspired by various elements such as the background, raised embroidery and trimmings, with the addition of beads, rings and frayed edges.

Just before going to press I received information from Avis Swann of Auckland, New Zealand, who was so inspired by the Casalguidi embroidery workshop in 1995 that she 'followed it up and visited Casalguidi where I met ladies still doing this wonderful work in their tiny village out from Florence. They were so surprised to meet someone so far away from them doing this type of embroidery. They embroidered linens for young ladies for their linen store!'

Avis was given three copies (a copy each for herself, her Embroiderers' Guild and me) of a recently published booklet titled *Il Ricamo di Casalguidi*, which celebrates the embroidery of Casalguidi following a recent successful exhibition. It contains a reprint of Adele Della Porta's 'Embroidery of Casalguidi—Practical and illustrated teaching guide', referred to on page 14, which was first published in 1915 by Sonzogno of Milan. Some of the designs featured in Della Porta's book are reflected in the photographs on pages 17, 65–69, 71 and 94.

A foreword by the Mayor of Serravalle Pistoiese refers to Casalguidi embroidery as 'this form of artistic craft which has always constituted a force to be considered within the economy of the region'; he says also, 'there were specialists who contributed directly to the dowries not only for country people but also for wealthy city families which was a tradition observed until only recently'. Even though fewer and fewer women dedicate themselves to this activity and the tradition of the dowry or trousseau has changed, there are still many requests for articles of household linen.

A presentation by Athos and Giordano Pratesi honours the heritage of 'fine embroidery, born in Casalguidi, and carried out by our grandmothers in their humble country homes. In the old days when our grandfathers sold Casalguidi embroidery at Livorno it would take them eight days, three days by horse to go there, two days to sell it and three days to come back'. The historical section by Federica Mabellini depicts a lion bag similar to those in the photos on pages 18 and 19 and in the diagram on page 14.

# HISTORICAL BACKGROUND

Casalguidi is a small Italian village near Pistoia, in Tuscany, north-west of Florence. There, in the late 1800s emerged a unique style of white embroidery which flourished until the beginning of World War I.

Italy has a rich history of white embroidery. Very early examples may be seen in paintings of the Renaissance period which provide many detailed depictions of embroidery such as female camisoles ornamented in reticella, the first needlemade lace developing from the cut-work of the 1500s. An example of reticella embroidery appears on page 12; the photo on the opposite page shows another type called *punto in aria* ('stitches in the air').

## Early whitework (linen-work)

Linen refers to and includes all the yarns and fabrics spun or woven from flax fibres. Early references mention linen work in ancient Egypt, Greece and other civilisations of the Mediterranean.

Cut-work embroidery is a specific type of needlework stitched onto a fabric of withdrawn threads. It embraces various forms of open-work and is seen as the link between embroidery and lace.

All the islands of the Aegean and Ionian seas formed part of the Byzantine empire (330–1453 AD) until the twelfth century. Greek threadwork has its origin in Byzantium which was renowned for its culture, art and crafts, particularly the textile arts. After the sack of Constantinople (now Istanbul) in 1204 by the soldiers of the Fourth Crusade, led by the Venetian Doge Enrico Dandolo, almost all the islands were ruled by Roman, Neapolitan, Sicilian, Genoese and above all Venetian overlords. Venice ruled almost exclusively in the Ionian islands, the Cyclades and Crete until the middle of the sixteenth century, when most of the Aegean came under Turkish jurisdiction.

The Greek Ionian Isles, in particular Corfu and Zante, were celebrated for a particular type of cut-work embroidery known as Greek lace which found its way to the shores of Italy.

Greek embroidery designs, once established on a certain island, appear to have been repeated almost stitch for stitch by succeeding generations.

The middle photo on page 12 shows a detail of a beautiful table runner hand stitched on the Greek island of Leros in the early twentieth century. A centre panel of cut-work is attached on both sides to bands of needlepoint lace and Cyprus embroidery, edged with bobbin lace.

The Folklore Museum at Argostoli on the island of Cephalonia contains a wealth of embroidered textiles with similarities to collections in Venetian museums. Cephalonia is the largest of the Ionian Islands and was under Byzantine rule until the thirteenth century, when it was taken over by the Venetians who ruled until the Empire fell in 1797.

Needlelace developing through drawn threadwork and cut-work made its first appearance in Venice at the end of the fifteenth century, moving to France in the middle of the sixteenth century and spreading throughout Europe.

After the fifteenth century cut-work and early lacemaking flourished in convents, at court and in the homes of the nobility. It occupied the time of ladies of high society who ornamented their fine linen with trimmings of cut-work and lace. Peasants also made and wore lace in a more practical way, ornamenting their shirts and hoods.

The Italian fashion of lace being worn by both men and women also found favour in the court of Elizabeth I of England where the ruffs were often made up of scallops of cut-work, which also decorated coverlets, cushions, handkerchiefs, cuffs and veils.

Italian pattern books by Antonio Taghiante (1528) and Nicolo d'Aristotile (1530) described in detail methods of making cut-work and needlemade lace identical with those used in the execution of Greek lace.

*Seventeenth century sampler 42 cm × 15 cm (16½″ × 6″). Bands of* punto in aria *('stitches in the air') with one unfinished band. Collection of the Embroiderers' Guild NSW Inc.*

In Italy during the 1500s a very large but fine camisole known as *camixa d'oro*, embroidered in gold thread and ornamented with pearls, was worn by wealthy ladies. Sumptuary laws prohibiting these very expensive items were continually ignored.

Counted thread embroidery on a background of squares, with heraldic flora and fauna designs incorporating arabesques, was developed as a pleasant pastime and worked by ladies living in palaces.

## Early lacemaking

Venice and the north of Italy continued to lead the field in needlepoint and lacemaking at the beginning of the seventeenth century. Venetian needlelace strongly influenced the needlelace of Spain, whose traders transported the laces to the Spanish and Portuguese colonies of South and Central America, the Philippines and the Canary Islands.

Lacemakers in England were also following the Venetian lead. In 1624 Richard Shorlayker produced *A Scholehouse for the Needle* which gave many designs following the Venetian influence, often incorporating a profusion of fruit, flowers and acorns. These designs, with the addition of human figures, insects, biblical themes, fantastic birds, castles and rural landscapes, all in bold colours, were the basis for the stumpwork craze which lasted from about 1660 to 1690. The stitches used in stumpwork were needlelace fillings worked over padding and sculptured wood. Casalguidi embroidery is sometimes described as resembling stumpwork.

In the early sixteenth century booklets and patterns for embroidery of German origin were published. Various designs including vases, dragons, sphinxes, lions, rabbits and other animals were later produced by a Mr Guadagnino. In Venice, the centre of the lace industry, booklets and magazines of stamped and traced designs for laces, point laces and fringes were produced in the second half of the sixteenth century. In the seventeenth and eighteenth centuries lace was used on camisoles and other articles.

## Nineteenth century revivals

In Italy in the nineteenth and early twentieth centuries the revival of embroidery in white was related not only to the increasing use of personal underwear and the increase in opulent and rich housing but also to the fact that underwear was more frequently washed. White was also considered a symbol of purity and chastity. Articles such as sheets, covers, towels, pillow shams, table cloths, doilies, nightshirts, underpants, stomachers, slips, blouses and handkerchiefs were embellished with embroidery.

*Seventeenth century reticella table cloth 130 cm × 136 cm (51¼" × 53½") with twelve matching napkins 36 cm (14¼") square. Note male and female motifs in the corners. Purchased in Florence in 1927. Collection of the Embroiderers' Guild NSW Inc.*

*Detail of linen table runner stitched by the late Maria Spanakides on the Greek island of Leros—early twentieth century. A centre panel of cut-work is attached on both sides to needlepoint lace which is attached to bands of Cyprus embroidery edged with bobbin lace. 304 cm × 80 cm (72" × 31"). Heirloom from the collection of Irene Mitrofanis.*

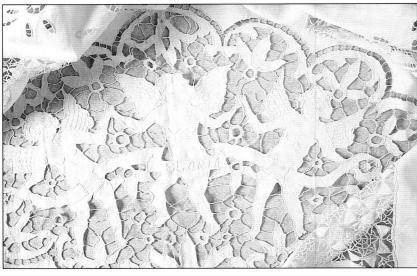

*Detail of an early twentieth century queen-size bedcover purchased in Sicily by the late Mrs E.M. Saducas. The centre depicts a popular cut-work motif of angels over a scroll containing the word* Gloria *('glorify'). The rest of the bedcover contains triangular insertions of reticella and bands of bobbin lace. Heirloom from the collection of Orestis Saducas.*

Italy was at the forefront of the use of lace and embroidery and fashion designers ornamented clothing with point lace, a fashion which remained in vogue for many decades.

Certain wealthy members of the Italian aristocracy, together with various writers and artists, supported the establishment of small companies and cooperatives in both major centres and country areas to create a revived industry in lace and embroidery. The products of this industry were sought after both in Italy and abroad.

Annual exhibitions displayed work created with needle and hoop, spindle and shuttle; the articles included bonnets, stomachers, shawls, aprons, camisoles and socks as well as all types of intimate underclothing and outer wear completely embroidered and embellished with unique rich laces. Fashion magazines promoted and popularised Palestrina (double knot) stitch and the pointed lace of Burano. Specialised embroidery manuals provided a wealth of ideas with instructions and designs in transfer form inspired by old textiles, paintings and architectural details. Designs featuring little flowers in a posy, ribbons, little baskets, roses, marguerites, peonies, violets, iris, tulips, carnations, hyacinths and ranunculi abounded. Statements and words of best wishes, felicity and good cheer appeared on some embroideries. The photograph at the foot of the opposite page shows a detail of a bedcover embroidered with words, the centre of which features angelic figures in cut-work embroidery joined by a scroll containing the word *Gloria* ('glorify'). In the early twentieth century there was great interest in pulled work and cut-work which also included insertions of filet lace, embroidery on fringes, more stylised motifs and geometric designs. All these elements, except for the embroidered fringe, are reflected in the bedcover. Pillow shams, curtains and bedcovers were covered with garlands tied with ribbons and hearts, trees with flowers or fruit and scenes of little animals and country vistas.

Old stitches from reticella and Venetian needlelace were revived. Specialised schools were established in Friuli, Venice, Turin, Liguria and Tuscany, Rome and Naples. The best known are l'Aemilia Ars in Bologna, the Industrie Femminili of Rome and the schools of Brazza and Fagagna.

In Pistoia, where the art of embroidery had been taught for centuries, silk weaving and embroidery were now taught at the Institute of the Abbandonate at Crocifissine as well as at the regional high school.

In the nearby village of Montorio near Quarrata there existed at the end of the nineteenth century a renowned school of needlelace managed by a noblewoman named Spaletti. In 1911 in the village of Lamporecchio a school called Merletti e Lavori Femminili ('lace and women's work') initiated a regular publication called *Ricamo di Lamporecchio* ('Embroidery of Lamporecchio').

The most sought after articles were items of intimate and domestic underwear requiring specialised handcrafting in small industrial enterprises, in particular family establishments specialising in machine embroidery and making up. Hand embroidery was sent to outworkers working in their homes.

These workers, who normally laboured in the fields or in the house, also embroidered piecework at home to increase their income. Others, mainly in large cities or villages, were able to spend most of their time embroidering.

Middlemen travelled around the country selling the products of long and patient work. Young girls learnt their first stitches from their mother or grandmother and then attended specialised schools, colleges or convents to learn more specialised embroidery.

The embroidery of Pistoia became better known after World War I and provided an important source of income for the area.

# CHARACTERISTICS OF TRADITIONAL CASALGUIDI EMBROIDERY

Verbal histories from the elderly embroiders of Casalguidi and Cantagrillo, recorded in the mid–1980s by Paolo Peri for an article on Casalguidi embroidery, give precious information on technique and style. The memories and personal experiences of these women verify the most typical original motifs produced in and around Casalguidi at Cantagrillo, Castel di Bobi, Baco di Sopra, Casenuove di Masiano and other small localities where experienced embroiderers operated in their homes to produce Casalguidi style embroidery. These specialist embroiderers gathered together in their backyards or on the street to work and exchange ideas and opinions; in this way their embroidery can also be seen as a form of socialising.

Casalguidi embroidery was later taught in a country school run by the Morelli sisters, which girls from adjacent localities also attended.

As were other well-known Italian embroideries, the Casalguidi style was promoted in a publication titled *Embroidery of Casalguidi—Practical and illustrated teaching guide* by Adele Della Porta.

## The designs

Innovative designs were inspired by the art of the Near East, the Far East, Africa and South America as well as by architectural elements from the external marblework of Pistoiese churches.

Among the most popular Casalguidi designs are those shown on the antique bag on page 2, two hexagons of padded raised stem band with Venetian rosettes in the centres, overcasting and buttonholed bars on a background of modified four-sided stitch, all trimmed with characteristic bobbles, and on pages 18–19.

The Lion of St Marks in Venice shows a close resemblance in its raised paw to the gestures of the embroidered lions.

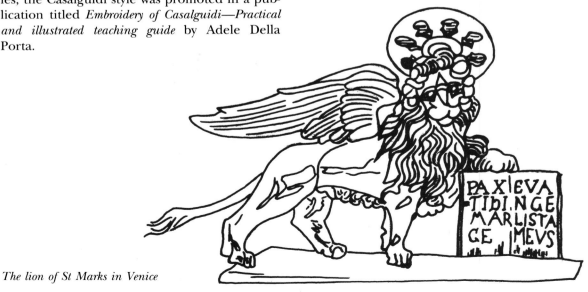

*The lion of St Marks in Venice*

*Detail of Casalguidi embroidery—a popular design of two hexagons of padded raised stem band with Venetian rosettes and overcasting on a background of modified four-sided stitch and trimmed with characteristic bobbles.*

Counted thread techniques were favoured to interpret geometric forms where the stitching achieves a very light and open effect. A less sophisticated but more closely characteristic version of this type of embroidery is shown in the diagram on this page where a series of squares interlock to form an open rhombus with a rosette in the centre and are surrounded by a band of withdrawn thread.

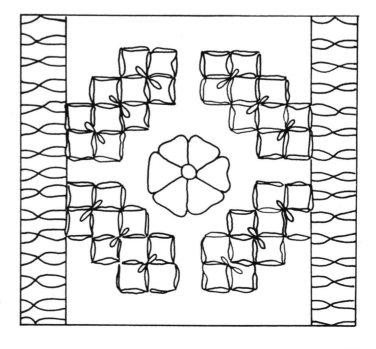

*Series of squares interlocking to form an open rhombus with a rosette in the centre and surrounded by bands of withdrawn thread*

A design called *a cappellino* was characterised by a square and rhombus in an ovoid form placed in the centre of a geometric figure surrounded by leaves and vine branches. It was usually worked without a background and surrounded with stylised ears of corn and flowers—see diagram below. Designs from the simplest to the most complex were enlivened or enriched by plant-like motifs such as those shown in the photograph on the opposite page in a delightful design featuring padded raised stem band, overcasting, buttonhole triangles, bullions and double buttonhole bars.

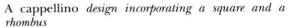

A cappellino *design incorporating a square and a rhombus*

Other designs used in Casalguidi represented the human figure. They were always worked on a background of withdrawn threads, with a typical motif being a man and a woman surrounded by flowers and vine leaves. Another motif represents a female figure joined to the fabric edges with buttonhole bars. These figures are reminiscent of the sculptures and prehistoric graffiti of some African tribes. They are also characteristic of the sculpture and bas-reliefs found in romantic and Gothic architecture.

Bird designs reminiscent of Byzantine and medieval bas-reliefs and mosaics were frequently used. They were often positioned in a square of withdrawn threads and the motif set in a diamond configuration joined together with vine leaves and tied with a corolla (the petals or inner floral leaves of a flower) as in the diagram below. Birds were popular designs in Byzantine textiles and the two-headed eagle which features in so many Greek threadworks was symbolic of Byzantium.

*Designs including human figures reminiscent of African art*

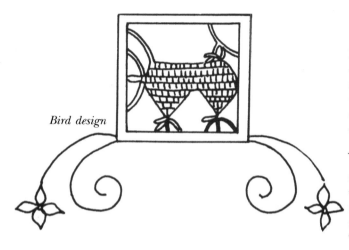

*Bird design*

*Detail of a sachet featuring Casalguidi embroidery worked in natural colours. Stitches are padded raised stem band (Casalguidi stitch), overcasting, buttonhole triangles, bullions and double buttonhole bars. 47 cm (18½") wide and 35 cm (13¾") long when folded in three. Collection of Wellington Embroiderers' Guild Inc. New Zealand.*

## The stitches

Padded raised stem band, or 'Casalguidi stitch', defines the classic look of the Casalguidi style, standing out in heavy relief to resemble sculptured marble. In the most characteristic form of Casalguidi embroidery, Casalguidi stitch is worked on a very light open background (*a jours*) made up on withdrawn threads of linen (*sfilato*) or on a four-sided or modified four-sided stitch (stitch Gayant). Open-work (*sfilato*) was created by cutting and withdrawing fabric threads while it was recommended that perle thread always be used to stitch the background. The four-sided or modified four-sided stitch (stitch Gayant) was worked following the same principle but without pulling the threads first—the threads had to be counted in groups of four to achieve a uniform result. Working in a frame gave the most even threadwork.

*Casalguidi lion bag 21 cm × 26 cm (8¼" × 10¼"), pink linen fabric worked with ecru linen thread. Italian, early twentieth century, from the collection of Valerie Carson, New Zealand.*

Even though many variations of the background have been used from time to time (created by pulling the threads, making it like a net, or applying a background of filet made by hand or machine onto the linen), the classic stitch of Casalguidi is made up on a background of four-sided or modified four-sided stitch (stitch Gayant).

After the background was prepared, the padded raised stem band (Casalguidi stitch) was worked onto it to produce the chosen design. Casalguidi stitch has been described as resembling 'a fine material like knitting which has a very pretty effect'. The embroidery was then ready for the spaces in between to be filled with secondary stitching of overcasting in perle thread. Depending on the subject being embroidered, the secondary stitching could be varied by using bullion stitch to interpret fruit

and grapes and single and double buttonhole bars for leaves. Another variation was to work additional openings onto the four-sided stitch with bars of wrapping, with or without picots, to create a Greek motif. Great precision in stitch placement gave the best results.

Another characteristic element of the Casalguidi style is the Venetian rosette, formed by six triangular petals of buttonhole stitch with only the foundation bars and the points of the triangles secured to the background to allow the petal to be raised and stand in relief.

Yet other characteristics of Casalguidi embroidery are the finishing details on articles such as cushions, curtains and bags—the bows and little balls (bobbles). The diagram on the next page shows an interesting example on an article described as a travel bag, where the background of four-sided stitch offsets the typical rosette in

*Pink linen bag decorated with Casalguidi work. Italian, early twentieth century, from the collection of The Embroiderers' Guild of Victoria, Melbourne.*

*Casalguidi travel bag trimmed with bobbles*

the centre surrounded with vines and leaves in overcasting, decorated with bobbles.

Another type of bobble was embellished with picots of bullion stitch on the sides, and little rings made into chains, in perle cotton. Sometimes bobbles were made by the crochet method.

Italian insertion stitch was used to join seams on articles such as cushions and bags, often finished with a hand-made cord. The cord was threaded through buttonholed loops, either plain or with picots as on the lion bags on these pages.

It was always recommended that perle thread be used and that stitch Gayant (four-sided or modified four-sided stitch) be worked on fabric held in a frame or hoop for best results.

*A profusion of colourful fabrics, threads, needles, scissors, frame and hoops.*

# MATERIALS AND TECHNIQUES

## Materials and equipment

The materials and equipment required for Casalguidi style embroidery are relatively few, and all are available from good craft departments, craft stores and mail order services. There are now many different types and colours of linen fabric and threads which have never before been available in such abundance.

### Embroidery thread

The most suitable threads for this work are DMC Coton perle nos. 3, 5, 8 and 12. Other suitable threads are DMC Coton à broder and flower thread, and the crochet threads Cébélia and Cordonnet special, nos. 5 to 40.

The thickness of the thread used will create different textures and weights of stitches. For example, coton perle no. 12 creates the finest result used on its own, but a different texture results when it is used in conjunction with coton perle nos. 8 and 5. DMC Cébélia crochet cotton is not quite as shiny as coton perle and produces a relatively mat finish.

Pure linen thread, available from specialist lace suppliers, gives a completely mat finish.

Also available are commercially produced space-dyed yarns which give a soft, random variation of colour. The Caron Collection produces 'Watercolours' and 'Wildflowers,' which are approximately the same thickness as no. 5 and no. 8 coton perle respectively but have a mat finish; Minnamurra Threads and Needle Necessities both produce a range of 'overdyed stranded' cottons to match colours in coton perle no. 8; Leah makes a range of overdyed coton perles in sizes 3, 5, 8 and 12.

Rainbow Threads supplies a brightly coloured range of embroidery linen thread. Pure linen yarns in various sizes are available from spinners and weavers' suppliers.

### Needles

Tapestry sizes 18–24 and crewel sizes 3–9 give a good range, while chenille needles, sizes 18–24, are better for thicker thread. Page 25 explains how to select the appropriate needle for your purpose.

### Scissors

Small sharp-pointed embroidery scissors for cutting fabric threads and embroidery threads. Large sharp fabric scissors for cutting fabric. Scissors for cutting paper. Hide your scissors from the rest of the family and don't use fabric scissors for cutting paper or any other purpose.

### Frame

A rectangular tapestry type frame provides better tensioning of fabric. The only limitation is that the project must fit within the frame.

### Embroidery hoop

Both rings of the hoop should be bound with bias binding to keep the work firm and clean. I find the 18 cm (7") hoop a good size to handle, giving easy access to the centre of the hoop and good control of tension.

### Evenweave fabric

Evenweave fabrics such as Belfast, Dublin, Quaker cloth, Edinburgh, Pastel, Cashel, Lugano and Floba by Zweigart and Scan Linen by Permin are all linen or linen mixtures suitable for Casalguidi style embroidery.

### Linen and linen mixtures

Zweigart specialises in manufacturing needlework fabrics. All the fabrics listed on page 24 are supplied in 140 cm (55") widths and a large colour range.

Permin of Copenhagen also manufactures needlework fabrics; their embroidery linen also comes in 140 cm (55") widths and a large colour range.

The fabric swatches on the following pages span the range of most colours available in Zweigart and Permin linens. The colour number and its description only is given as well as the closest DMC stranded cotton colour

Zweigart linens

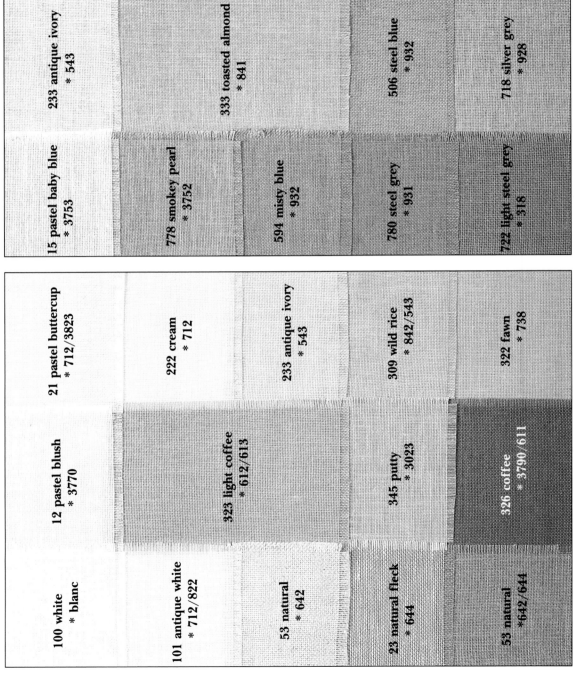

Zweigart linens

100 white
* blanc

101 antique white
* 712/822

53 natural
* 642

23 natural fleck
* 644

53 natural
*642/644

21 pastel buttercup
* 712/3823

222 cream
* 712

233 antique ivory
* 543

309 wild rice
* 842/543

322 fawn
* 738

12 pastel blush
* 3770

323 light coffee
* 612/613

345 putty
* 3023

326 coffee
* 3790/611

15 pastel baby blue
* 3753

778 smokey pearl
* 3752

594 misty blue
* 932

780 steel grey
* 931

722 light steel grey
* 318

16 pastel mint
* 964

233 antique ivory
* 543

333 toasted almond
* 841

506 steel blue
* 932

718 silver grey
* 928

718 silver grey
* 928

774 blue violet
* 341

596 powder blue
* 322

781 cobblestone
* 646

* Denotes nearest DMC stranded cotton colour number to match fabric

Colours available in Zweigart fabrics shown with colour number and name. Not all colours are available in each type of fabric.

**Permin linens**

27 dusty green * 524

114 apple blossom * 224

39 antique tan * 543

111 desert sand * 738

28 English rose * 3743

25 plum blossom * 3041

77 silvery moon * 932

113 star sapphire * 3753/3756

36 antique blue * 932

37 antique green * 503

76 prairie grain * 3013

131 wild raspberry * 902

38 antique lavender * 3042

78 autumn leaf * 783

24 blue wing * 926

132 lavender mist * 327

*Some of the colours available in Permin linen shown with colour number and name.*

**Zweigart linens**

345 putty * 3023

638 olive green * 523

641 dark teal green * 500

610 sage * 503

403 antique pink * 224/778

41 pastel peach * 225

484 cameo rose * 225

483 mulberry * 3726

14 pastel pink * 778

474 light plum * 3042

720 black * 310

*Denotes nearest DMC stranded cotton colour number to match fabric.*

23

**Zweigart needlework fabrics**

| Item no. | Name | Threads per inch | Threads per cm | Composition |
|---|---|---|---|---|
| 3217 | Edinburgh | 36 | 16 | 100% linen |
| 3609 | Belfast | 30 | 12 | 100% linen |
| 3604 | Dublin | 25 | 10 | 100% linen |
| 3993 | Quaker | 28 | 11 | 55% lin/45% cott |
| 3281 | Cashel | 28 | 11 | 100% linen |
| 3234 | Pastel | 28 | 11 | 48% lin/52% cott |
| 3835 | Lugana | 25 | 10 | 52% cott/48% viscose |
| 3988/53 | Floba | 25 | 10 | 30% lin/70% viscose |
| 1198/53 | Floba | 18 | 6 | 30% lin/70% viscose |

**Permin needlework fabrics**

| Item no. | Name | Threads per inch | Threads per cm | Composition |
|---|---|---|---|---|
| 065 | Linen | 32 | 13 | 100% linen |
| 076 | Linen | 28 | 11 | 100% linen |

number for easy identification. These colours may not be available in all types of fabric and you will have to check with suppliers as to which colours are available in a particular fabric.

## Glossary of basic techniques

**Cutting linen fabrics and preparing for stitching**
Allow more fabric than you think you need, adding 8 cm (3") all around the finished size of the article plus hems.

The first step is to withdraw one thread of fabric on the line to be cut—this clearly shows the straight grain. Use a sharp pair of scissors

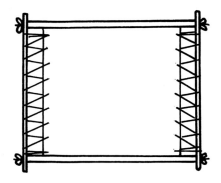

*Linen fabric laced into a rectangular wooden frame*

to cut on the grain of the fabric. Overlock or zigzag stitch the edge to prevent fraying.

Use a hoop to hold the fabric firm while stitching or attach the overlocked fabric to a rectangular wooden frame. Attach the two sides to the cotton tape of the rollers with a running stitch using thick embroidery thread, or use a wide, open, machine zigzag stitch. Lace the other two sides of the fabric to the frame with loops of thick crochet or embroidery yarn no more than 2.5 cm (1") apart. Refer to the photograph on page 20 and the diagram.

Use one continuous length of yarn for each side; don't cut the yarn off the skein or ball until the side is completely laced.

**'Not through fabric'**
These words are used throughout the book to indicate that the needle and thread are not taken through the fabric to form the particular stitch.

**Tension and ease of stitching**
One of the most important aims of an embroiderer is to achieve a constant stitch tension.

The left thumb for right-handers (right thumb for left-handers) is an invaluable aid as a stabiliser to control thread movement. Hold the thread with the thumb of the non-stitching hand in such a position that the stitching area is clear, thus making the insertion of needle and thread by the stitching hand much easier. At the same time the stitching hand is pulling the thread after each movement to create the tension. Don't pull the tension in one movement; most especially, do not exert the pull a long way from the fabric, particularly not from shoulder level or beyond. Pulling from the end of the thread creates uneven tension as the tension must be adjusted as the thread becomes shorter.

The best way is to adjust the tension in two movements, first to loosely pull the thread into position, then pulling the correct degree of tension close to the stitch itself. With practice you will automatically pull an even tension and become aware that it can be pulled loose, medium or tight in varying degrees to best suit a particular stitch, its purpose and ease of execution.

Throughout the book reference is made to the degree of tension required to achieve a better result for the stitch and its effect.

### Starting and finishing a thread
A new thread is woven back and forth in the back of the work to start and finish off. When there is no embroidery, use a waste knot to start stitching.

### Waste knot
This is a very tidy and useful way to begin stitching onto fabric where there is no existing embroidery.

Make a knot in the end of the thread and take the needle and thread through the front of the fabric 4 cm (1½") away from the first stitch. After the embroidery stitches have been worked, cut off the knot and weave the tail of thread into the back of the work. When starting four-sided stitch always insert the needle and knotted thread through the front of the fabric 4 cm (1½") away from the first stitch as described above. Lay the tail of any new thread at the back of the work in line with the first row of stitching so that it is stitched over and secured. Cut off the waste knot after stitching over the tail of thread.

Always finish each thread at the back before starting to embroider with a new thread so you don't have loose threads hanging at the back while you work.

### Lock stitch
The buttonhole stitch or half hitch is used as a 'stopper' to lock other stitches into place to prevent loosening or unravelling.

### Needles
Never use rusty needles—throw them away! Prevent rusting by storing packets of needles in an airtight container and single needles in a needlebook of doctor flannel or felt. The right needle for the purpose makes the embroidery easier and results in a better finish. Choose the right size for the thickness of thread used and the right type, i.e. pointed or blunt end, to suit the thread, fabric and stitch.

As a general guide I use a size 26 tapestry needle for no. 12 perle and size 24 for nos. 5 and 8 perle and 6 strands of stranded cotton.

Use a crewel needle with a sharp point where weaving isn't used, and a tapestry needle (blunt point) for weaving or for detached buttonhole stitch.

Bullion knots are easier to work using a milliner's needle. The size with the largest eye, no. 1, takes 6 strands of stranded cotton.

If the needle is not passing easily through the fabric and is causing thread damage, change to a larger needle which will create a hole in the fabric big enough to allow the thread to pass through it without fraying. Another way to minimise thread damage is to change the position of the needle on the thread from time to time.

### Crewel needles
Have a sharp point and are available in the same size range as sharps, i.e. nos. 3–9, the smallest number referring to the largest size; these needles have a long narrow eye to carry the thread and facilitate ease of passage through the fabric with minimum thread irritation.

### Sharps needles
For general purpose sewing. Their short round eyes provide added strength. Sizes 3–9 are the most popular (again the smaller the number the larger the size).

### Tapestry needles
Have a large eye and a blunt end and come in sizes 16–26 (again, the smaller the number the larger the size). Tapestry needles are ideal for

use on linen embroidery where the needle must separate the fabric threads and pass through the holes of the fabric. They are used with pulled thread background stitches such as four-sided stitch and its variations, as well as for needlelace, buttonhole stitches, wrapping and raised stem band stitch.

### Chenille needles

Have the same characteristics and numbers as tapestry needles except that they have a sharp point. They are useful when a sharp pointed needle is required to carry thicker yarn.

### Milliner's needles

Much longer than the abovementioned needles; their round eye doesn't curve out beyond the width of the needle so that the sides form smooth lines. This characteristic makes them ideal for bullion stitch as the wrapping of the bullion stitch isn't resisted by a bulge. Their only disadvantage is that the eye isn't very big, which limits the thickness of thread used. The largest size is no. 1, which takes up to 6 strands of stranded cotton.

### Beading needles

Very long and fine with a small eye enabling them to pass through small bead-holes. The length of the needle makes it easier to pick up and thread a number of beads at one time.

### Transferring the design to fabric

Accurate transfer of the design is critical to the success of the embroidery. Transfer the design *after* the pulled thread background has been worked onto the fabric.

When you transfer the design you may not need to draw in every detail. For example, a flower made from buttonhole bars, single or double, could be transferred as a single directional line only, as the stitch will fill the shape shown on the pattern. The diagram shows that tracing over the dotted lines will provide an adequate outline.

I recommend two methods for transferring the design:

**1. Tacking around a cut-out paper shape** This is the easiest method but its use is limited to a certain type of design; for example, the eucalyptus design on page 80, the butterfly design on page 84 and the cornflower tissue box cover on page 96 could be transferred, wholly or in part, by this method.

Trace the outlines of the whole design onto greaseproof or soft tracing paper and pin it to the fabric. Cut out sections of the traced design as you run-stitch next to the edge of the cut paper with a sharps or crewel needle, using contrasting coloured sewing cotton. Alternatively, cut out the shapes carefully with a pair of paper scissors, position them on the fabric with pins and tack small running stitches around them. Ensure that corners are easily identifiable by adding extra stitches where necessary.

**2. Stitch and tear method** After tracing the design onto greaseproof or soft tracing paper pin it to the fabric and run-stitch the design with bright contrasting coloured sewing cotton, through the paper and fabric together, being careful to add extra stitches to indicate points and details.

Carefully tear off the paper a little at a time. This is easier if you first run the sharp point of the needle around the run-stitched design.

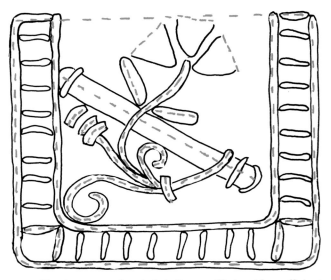

*Tracing over the dotted lines will provide sufficient outline*

# *Handy hints*

### A single thread in the needle
This is easier to control than a double thread. If a double thread is needed always use two single lengths threaded together through the needle. Never use a single thread doubled over.

### Surface embroidery worked on an open background
Surface embroidery worked on an open background of four-sided stitch will often require that the needle be inserted into a hole. *Don't* take the needle *through* the hole, as this will pull the stitch through to the back—instead, catch the thread on the edge of the four-sided stitching.

### Combing tassel skirts
Comb a tassel skirt with a tapestry needle after it is made to organise the threads into place.

### Removing kinks in tassel skirts
Take out kinks in the skirt of a tassel by steaming the tassel above boiling water, holding it with long-handled tongs to avoid burns. Comb the threads of the skirt with a tapestry needle.

### Running out of thread
Should your thread run out before you have finished buttonhole stitching the head of the tassel, leave the tail-end of the yarn hanging while you thread a new needle and yarn up through the skirt, bringing it out through the same hole as the tail of yarn. Continue with the new thread, going back later to finish off the tail-end by taking it down to blend in the skirt.

### Lock stitch
The buttonhole stitch or half stitch is used as a 'stopper' to lock other stitches into place to prevent loosening or unravelling.

### Fraying metallic thread
Divisible metallic thread tends to fray, but this can be effectively prevented by applying a small amount of craft glue to approximately 1 cm (⅜") of both ends of the length of yarn, then pinching the ends to form points.

### Ladder stitch
Ideal for joining two edges together without stitches showing.

### Increasing and decreasing buttonhole stitches
To increase, work two stitches into every second stitch of the previous round. In the next round work one stitch in every stitch of the previous round. Repeat this as necessary.

To decrease work one stitch into every second stitch of the previous round, or as necessary to maintain even spacing.

The definitive characteristic of *punto Casalguidi* is the contrast between a heavy relief which resembles sculptured marble worked on a very light open background (*à jours*) made up on withdrawn threads of linen (*sfilato*) or on a four-sided or modified four-sided stitch (stitch Gayant).

*Experiments with four-sided stitch worked on the back and front of Floba linen with DMC* Fil or clair *and no. 8 coton perle yarns after withdrawing fabric threads. This panel would be most attractive as part of a blouse.*

# BACKGROUND STITCHES

## Opening up the background

Before stitching the raised elements of Casalguidi style embroidery the background fabric is opened up with four-sided stitch. There are three ways to do this:

1: Four-sided stitch worked straight onto the fabric.
2: Four-sided stitch worked on a grid of withdrawn threads for a lacy, more open effect.
3: Modified four-sided stitch worked straight onto the fabric or a grid of withdrawn threads.

### Materials

Evenweave linen 11–13 threads per cm (26–32 threads per inch)
DMC coton perle no. 8 or 12, or 2 strands stranded cotton
Tapestry needle size 24
Hoop or frame

## Method 1: Four-sided stitch

Start 4 cm (1½") away from the first stitch with a waste knot at the front of the work (see page 25) as shown in the diagram over the page so that the stitching will be worked over it.

Each stitch is worked over 4 threads of fabric.

Snip off the waste knot when you have stitched to it. Finish off by taking the thread under the stitches at the back, taking care not to allow it to show through.

*Right-handed stitch:* A-B-C, C-A-D, D-B-C, repeat to end of row.

*Left-handed stitch:* A-B-C, C-A-D, D-B-C, repeat to end of row.

Turn the work around and commence the next row under the last stitch.

## Method 2: Four-sided stitch on a grid of withdrawn threads

Tack-mark the shape to be stitched with sewing cotton. Find the midway point of a horizontal thread within the shape and cut it with a small

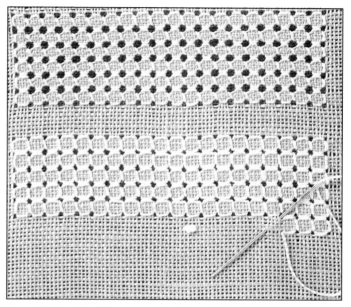

*Four-sided stitch: The top section is worked with tight tension and the bottom with loose tension.*

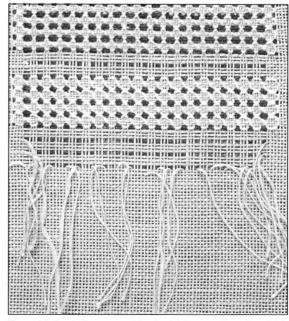

*Four-sided stitch on a grid of withdrawn threads which are shown being withdrawn. The top section is worked with tight tension and the bottom with loose tension.*

Right handed

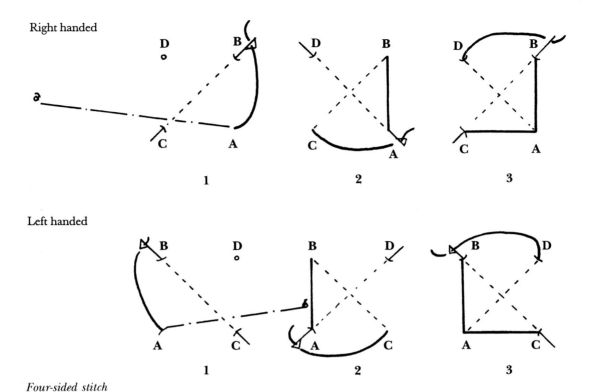

Left handed

*Four-sided stitch*

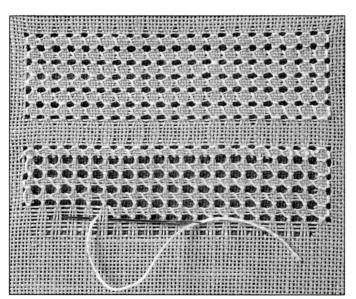

*Modified four-sided stitch: The top section is worked with medium tension straight onto the fabric and the bottom is worked with tight tension on a grid of withdrawn threads.*

pair of sharp-pointed scissors. Withdraw the horizontal thread with a tapestry needle to both sides of the shape, stopping four threads before the tacked line. Cut the withdrawn thread.

Withdraw every fourth horizontal thread in the same way.

Repeat the procedure for every fourth vertical thread to create a clear open grid which enables easy working of four-sided stitch.

Stitch four-sided stitch from tack-marked line to tack-marked line following the diagrams above. Each stitch is worked over 3 threads of fabric. **Note: A four-sided stitch extending beyond the cut thread is adequate to lock it.**

### Method 3: Modified four-sided stitch

Prepare the fabric using method 1 or 2 on page 29.
*Row 1:* Work four-sided stitch, as above.
*Row 2:* Turn work upside down and working from right to left, A-B-C, C-B-D, repeat to end of row, following the first two diagrams on the next page.
*Row 3:* Turn work around again and work from right to left, A-B-C, C-A-C, following the third and fourth diagrams on the next page.

Repeat rows 2 and 3 *only* alternately to the end of the shape.

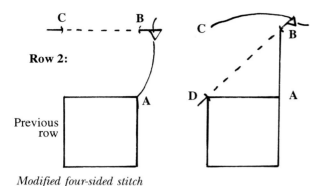

Row 2:

Previous row

*Modified four-sided stitch*

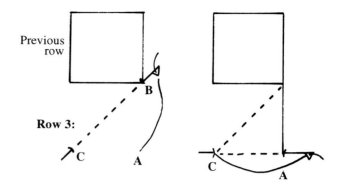

Previous row

Row 3:

## Designing the shape of the open background

The open background may cover the whole area of the project, or it may form a border, a feature square, a feature rectangle or any shape you can imagine.

The textures of the plain unworked fabric contrasted with the open work makes an attractive pattern of rough and smooth.

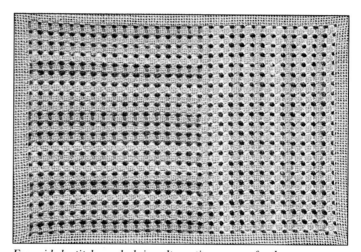

*Four-sided stitch worked in alternating rows of colour using coton perle no. 8, colours ecru, 3042 light antique mauve, 3041 dark antique mauve, 644 light green beige, 503 antique green light, 948 pink on Belfast fabric colour light plum.*

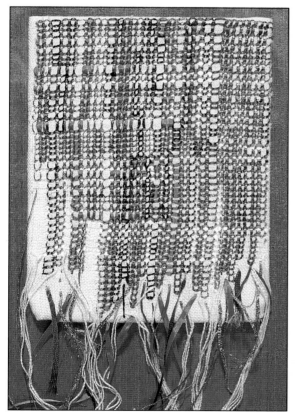

*Experiments with four-sided stitch worked in vertical bands of ribbon and gold yarns on an uneven grid of withdrawn threads of Floba fabric.*

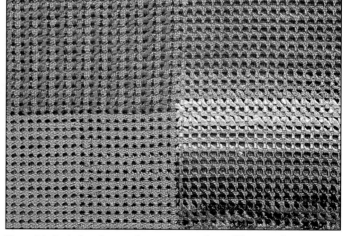

*Four-sided stitch using various yarns such as ribbons and metallics which have the effect of making the background more dominant.*

Each stitch creates a statement of texture, either patterned and rough or quite smooth. It is this contrast combined with padded raised stem band and the open background which gives the Casalguidi style its fascinating surface.

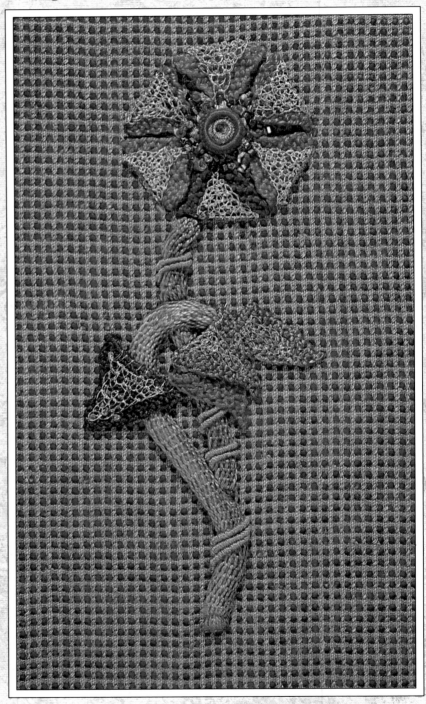

'Golden Rosette' by Pamela Gordon: padded raised stem band, bullions, French knots, buttonholed rings and two layers of buttonhole stitched triangles.

# REPERTOIRE OF SURFACE STITCHES

Surface stitches are embroidered after the fabric has been prepared with an open-work background (page 29) and the design transferred to the fabric (page 26).

The stitches in the first group are based on buttonhole stitch—single and double buttonhole bars, space fillers, triangles and Venetian rosette. All these stitches create a patterned rough surface.

Bullion stitch gives a smooth surface as do curl, overcasting and wrapping.

Padded raised stem band can be either rough or smooth depending on its neighbouring stitches.

Woven picot, a popular stitch in Venetian needlelace and stumpwork, is not seen in traditional Casalguidi embroidery but is included because of its texture and flexibility and its resemblance to buttonhole stitch triangles.

## Single buttonhole bars

These may be used to form small or large rectangular shapes or to form curves. A variation is shown on the eight-petalled flower where each petal is made of two rows of buttonhole stitch on one side of the bar (shown in the photo).

Belfast fabric colour 233 antique ivory
DMC coton perle no. 8:
    ecru
    503 blue green medium
    504 blue green light

As shown over the page, make two firm straight stitches between two points 12 mm (½") apart and bring the needle and thread out 3 mm (⅛") away from one end at A. Buttonhole stitch around the two bars, not through the fabric, using firm tension to the end, and take needle

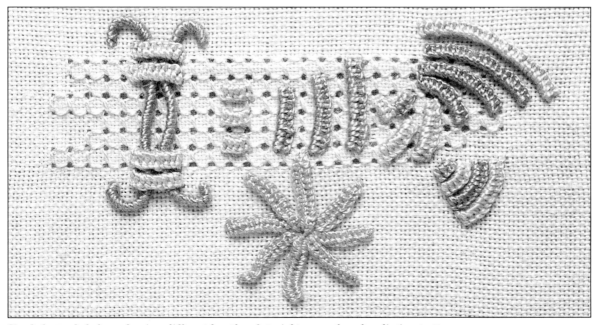

*Single buttonhole bars showing different lengths of straight, curved and radiating patterns.*

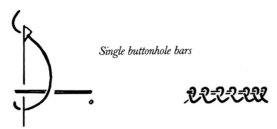

*Single buttonhole bars*

and thread into the fabric 3 mm (⅛") away from the bars at B. This forms a rectangular shape. To curve the bars loosen the tension on the two straight stitches at the beginning. The curve may be stitched into place with matching sewing cotton. Parallel lines of bars form a very attractive shape filler.

## Double buttonhole bars

Dublin fabric colour 322 fawn
DMC stranded cotton:
   738 tan very light
DMC coton perle no. 8:
   356 terracotta medium
   918 red copper dark
DMC coton perle no. 5:
   503 blue green medium
   504 blue green light

This stitch is similar to single buttonhole bars except that two rows of buttonhole stitch are

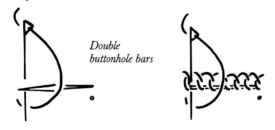

*Double
buttonhole bars*

worked over the bars, one on either side. Make two straight stitches in the same holes, bring the needle and thread out 2–3 mm (1/10") away from one corner and buttonhole stitch over the two bars with medium tension. Don't pack in too many as the same number of stitches is to be fitted on the other side of the bar. Finish off this row by taking the needle and thread into the fabric 2–3 mm (1/10") away. Bring the needle out 2–3 mm (1/10") away from the end of the bar on the other side, turn the work around and buttonhole stitch between each stitch of the first row and over the bars, using medium tension. Finish off at the same distance from the bar at the end of the second row.

## Buttonhole stitch space filler

Belfast fabric colour 333 toasted almond
DMC stranded cotton 407 sportsman flesh dark
   for four-sided stitch (2 strands)
DMC coton perle no. 5 598 turquoise light
DMC coton perle no. 8 341 blue violet light

1. Work small back stitches onto the fabric around the shape to be filled.
2. Commence buttonhole stitch on one side of the shape, working the first row through the back stitches, not through the fabric. Finer thread may require more than one buttonhole stitch in each back stitch. Work straight rows of buttonhole stitch from left to right, then right to left. At the beginning and end of each row pick up a back stitch with a buttonhole stitch.
3. Finish the last row with buttonhole stitches, picking up together a stitch from the previous row and one of the remaining back stitches.

*Centre—double buttonhole bars; left—double buttonhole bars with another row worked on one row of stitches; right—double buttonhole bars with another row added to both sides.*

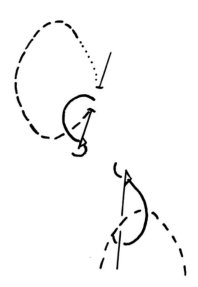

*Buttonhole stitch space filler: The example on the right is attached to the fabric only on its left edge.*

To increase buttonhole stitches work two stitches in every second stitch of the previous row.

To decrease buttonhole stitches work a stitch in every second stitch or as dictated by the shape.

All the buttonhole stitches are worked above the surface of the fabric; the only time the needle and thread go through the fabric is at the beginning and end of each new thread which is always finished and started at the end of a row.

Buttonhole stitch space filler may be raised by padding it with the same thread used for stitching. Wind a length of thread around your

*Steps in buttonhole stitch space filler*

finger, remove it and push it in through a gap before completing the shape. Refer to the diagram above.

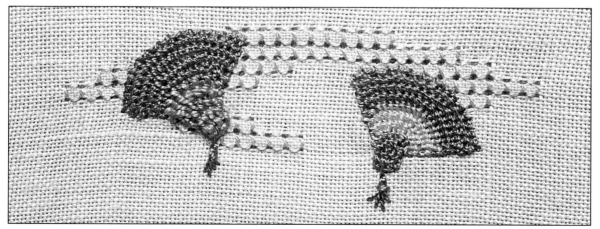

*Buttonhole stitch space filler, with return* (see next page)

35

### Buttonhole stitch space filler, with return

Belfast fabric colour 3609/309 wild rice
DMC stranded cotton 407 sportsman flesh dark
   for four-sided stitch (2 strands)
DMC coton perle no. 8:
   3041 antique violet medium
   758 terracotta very light
   931 antique blue medium

1. Work small back stitches around the shape to be filled (diagram A).
2. Referring to diagram B, bring needle out at A and take the thread across to B under a back-stitch but not through the fabric—this is called a return.

*Buttonhole stitch space filler, with return*

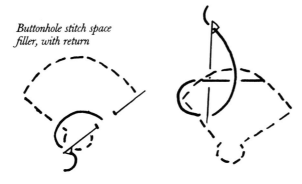

3. Work a row of buttonhole stitches from left to right, taking the thread through a backstitch made in step 1 together with the return, not through the fabric.
4. Without stitching through the fabric take the thread around a backstitch on the right under the previous row, back across the shape and under a backstitch on the left side to create another return.
5. Buttonhole stitch from left to right, taking the thread into a stitch in the previous row and the return created in step 4.

Repeat steps 4 and 5 until the shape is filled, repeating step 3 for the last row and working all stitches above the surface of the fabric.

Follow instructions above for increasing, decreasing and padding.

### Buttonhole stitch triangles

Buttonhole stitch triangles are a characteristic feature of Casalguidi style. Use them traditionally or play with the triangular shape in different geometric arrangements, manipulate them or overlap them. The triangle is joined to the fabric in only two places, at the foundation bars at the beginning and at the point. Until you are confident with this stitch, work each triangle separately—if there's a problem you can cut the mistake off instead of having to unpick it.

Belfast fabric 484 cameo rose
DMC stranded cotton 316 antique mauve
   medium for four-sided sitch (2 strands)
DMC coton perle no. 5 807 peacock blue
Minnamurra coton perle no. 8 170 peacock/
   violet

Count the number of stitches in each row as you work to ensure you have made the correct number to guarantee the triangular shape. This stitch is easier to work in coton perle no. 5 or 8 using a size 24 tapestry needle.

Commence the triangles by making two straight stitches between two points to form foundation bars and bring the needle and thread out again through one point.
*Row 1:* Make eight or more buttonhole stitches around the foundation bars, not through the fabric.
*Row 2:* Working in the opposite direction to row 1 make another row of buttonhole stitches into the first row, again not working through fabric. There are two less stitches in row 2 than row 1.
*Row 3 to end of triangle:* Buttonhole stitch into

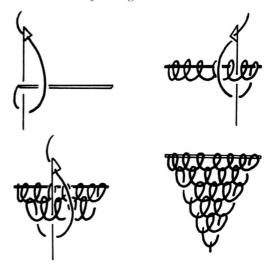

*The buttonhole triangle does not necessarily sit flat on the fabric; traditionally it is manipulated to sit above the surface.*

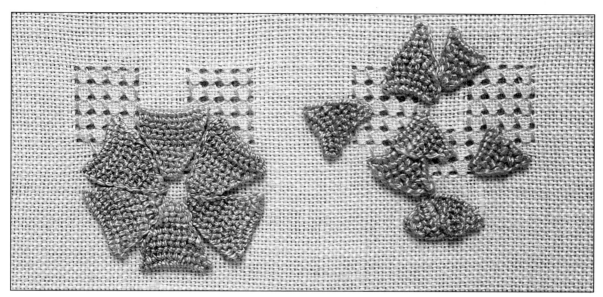

*Venetian rosette and buttonhole stitch triangles*

the preceding row, not through fabric, decreasing by one stitch and continuing until only one stitch remains. Position the triangle and anchor it by stitching the tail of thread at the point through the fabric, securing it at the back of the work.

*Important:* After row 2 the number of stitches in *each row* decreases by *one stitch* only to the end.

## Venetian rosette

The Venetian rosette, another distinctive feature of Casalguidi embroidery, contains six buttonhole stitch petals worked within a hexagonal shape. The foundation bars of each triangular petal are stitched down a small distance in from the corners of the hexagon to achieve a rounded shape as shown in the diagram.

1. Transfer a hexagonal shape to the fabric with running stitches. Each side of the hexagon in the sample is 2.5 cm (1") long; a small diamond shape is left in the centre to show where the triangles are attached to the fabric and to allow for the finishing touch of curl stitches.
2. Work one buttonhole stitch triangle attached to each side of the hexagon, commencing with foundation bars 3 mm (⅛") in from the corners of the hexagon and starting with ten or more buttonhole stitches, depending on the size of the hexagon and the thickness of the thread. Each triangle of the Venetian rosette in the photo was worked on fifteen stitches.

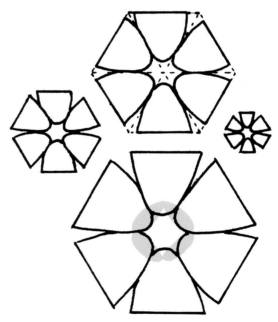

*Note: An easy way to draw perfect hexagons is to use isometric graph paper, available from specialist stationery suppliers.*

3. Do not stitch the triangles down at the centre yet, placing each one out of the way until all six have been made. Now secure the triangles, rounding the points as shown in the diagram.
4. Four curl stitches (refer to page 42) are then stitched in the centre to form the diamond shape shown in colour on the diagram but omitted from the stitch sample.

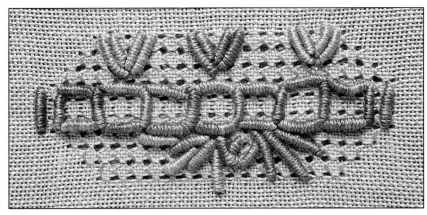

*Bullion stitch*

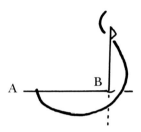

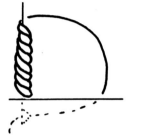
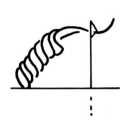

## Bullion stitch

Quaker fabric 474 light plum
DMC stranded cotton 316 antique mauve
  medium for four-sided stitch (2 strands)
DMC stranded cotton:
  3041 antique violet medium
  316 antique mauve
Minnamurra coton perle no. 8 8130 mauve/
  violet
Milliner's needle, size 1

The milliner's needle takes 6 strands of
stranded cotton and is excellent for making a
smooth even bullion stitch; some threads, e.g.
stranded cotton, are easier to use in a bullion
knot than others.

1. Following the diagram, bring needle and
thread out at A and insert again at B; don't pull
all the thread through but hold it with your left
hand (left-handers please reverse).
2. Place right hand under fabric and push
needle out of fabric at A until nearly all of the
needle is visible. Keep hold of the needle. With
the left hand wind the thread around the
needle 8 or more times as desired, using the
right hand to hold and turn the needle to assist
the winding. Wind the thread with even tension
around the thicker part of the needle, neither
too tightly nor too loosely.

3. Hold wound thread and needle firmly with
the left hand and with the right hand pull the
needle gently through the coils. While pulling
the needle and thread through, loosen your
hold on the needle a little and push the coils
lightly in the opposite direction to the way they
are wrapped. This has the effect of loosening
the threads and allowing the needle to pull
through more easily. Tease the coils with the
needle while firming the coiled stitch by pulling
the thread. Insert needle at B again to anchor
the stitch.

## Stem stitch

Stem stitch in Casalguidi embroidery is used as
a foundation for overcasting stitch.

It is also stitched over foundation bars in
raised stem band.

*Stem stitch*

## Padded raised stem band

Padded raised stem band, the most distinctive feature of Casalguidi embroidery, is referred to as Casalguidi stitch. Traditionally it was worked very finely with the foundation bars quite close together, and then decorated with long bullion stitches which enhance and modify the strong statement of unbroken raised stem band. Traditionally, bullion knots were often strategically placed over the corners and ends of raised stem band, not only enhancing the padded raised stem band and effectively breaking up and sub- duing a very strong line, but also covering problem points.

Belfast fabric colour 483 mulberry
DMC coton perle no. 8:
    3042 antique violet light
    776 pink medium
Minnamurra no. 8 perle 8130 mauve/violet
crewel needle size 3 or 5
tapestry needle size 24

1. Make thread padding by cutting off 10 lengths no. 8 (or 7 lengths no. 5) coton perle, each double the length of the line to be embroi- dered plus 10 cm (4") for handling. Fold the bunch of threads in half and sew the looped end to one end of the design line with two stitches in sewing cotton. Refer top row photo.
2. Stitch the padding to the design line with couching stitches in sewing cotton, bringing needle and thread out on the design line, taking it around the thread padding and back through the same hole. Couching stitches are 6–12 mm (¼"–½" apart) and tension should be medium, not tight, so that a smooth tubular shape is formed. Before reaching the end of the design finish the ends of the padding by taking a second crewel needle and sewing cotton and stitching and wrapping the threads securely together. Cut off excess padding threads and continue couching to the end of the design line.
3. Cover the thread padding with satin stitch using either matching or contrasting coloured thread and a crewel needle—no. 5 coton perle (or six strands of stranded cotton) for speed, or no. 8 coton perle (or 3 strands of stranded cotton) for a finer result. There is no need to take the needle in and out the same hole as in step 2. (Second row of photo.)

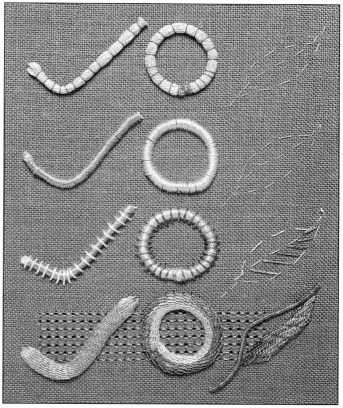

*Padded raised stem band*
*Top row: left and centre—thread padding couched to the fabric; right—outline for unpadded raised stem band.*
*Second row: left and centre—thread padding covered with satin stitch; right—outline for unpadded raised stem band.*
*Third row: left and centre—foundation stitches made over satin-stitched thread padding; right—foundation stitches laid in preparation for unpadded raised stem band.*
*Fourth row: Raised stem band stitched onto the founda- tion bars. The leaf shape is finished with a line of wrapping.*

4. Foundation stitches are now made over the satin-stitched thread padding at intervals of approximately 5 mm (¼"). These bars should be of medium tension, not tight, as many rows of stem stitch will pass over and around them. The foundation bars are placed at a right angle to the line of padding. Curved lines require the bars to radiate around the curves so that the line of raised stem stitch will curve smoothly. Foundation bars placed right on the end of the

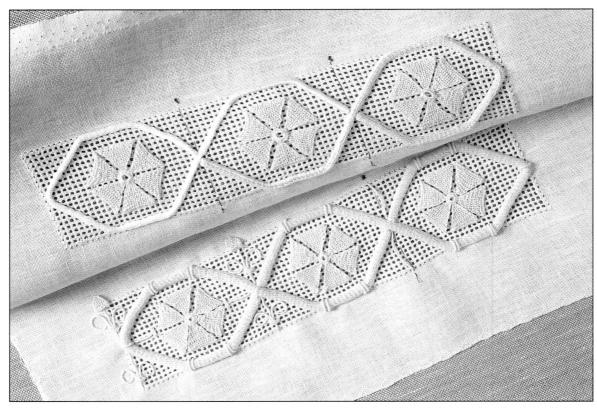

*The three steps of padded raised stem band are clearly shown on the hexagons worked on both ends of a table centre by Lynne Leighton.*

padding will slip off, so keep the end bars in a few millimetres. When you've had some practice with this stitch try working the foundation bars closer together for a very fine result and almost total coverage of the padding. (Third row of photo.)

5. Work stem stitch over the foundation bars in rows using a tapestry needle, taking one stitch over each bar created in step 4. Stitch only in one direction, left to right.

Start working on the row furthest away from you, with subsequent rows worked toward you for ease of working. Each row starts and finishes at each end approximately 5 mm (¼") out from the padding. Some rows may start or finish in the same hole as a previous row to allow them to sit straight. As you complete each row push it with a tapestry needle towards the previous one to pack them firmly together. Avoid splitting the thread of the foundation bars with the raised stem stitch as this will make it impossible to move the row to pack it close to the previous one. Finish off each row individually and start

each subsequent row with a new thread. Make sure the ends of the padded stem stitch roll are neat with stitches evenly spaced. (Fourth row of photo.)

**Circular shapes** The first row of raised stem stitch is worked on the outside of the circle. Tack a line of running stitch on the background fabric next to the first raised stem band stitch to indicate the start/finish point.

**Curves and corners** Take care here with your tension to create an even surface of stitches. Some corners are more difficult than others to cover; sometimes a shorter, extra compensating row of raised stem stitch may be required to fill the gap.

**Finishing and starting off threads in the middle of a row of raised stem band** Should your thread run out before you have finished a row, particularly in a continuous circle, leave the end of the yarn unfinished while you thread a new needle and yarn between the padding and previous raised stem band stitching. Continue stitching with the new thread and then go back and finish off the remaining short length, taking it to the back of the fabric between the padding and previous stitching.

## Woven bars

Woven bars in rectangular and leaf shapes, as seen in the photo below, are used extensively in traditional Casalguidi embroidery.

Permin fabric colour 131 wild raspberry
DMC stranded cotton 316 antique mauve for four-sided stitch (2 strands)
DMC coton perle no. 5:
    931 antique blue medium
    932 antique blue light
Minnamurra no. 8 perle 8240 blue/violet

### Rectangular woven bars

Make two straight stitches parallel to each other and approximately 3 mm (⅛") apart. Bring the needle out at the beginning of one of the bars and weave backwards and forwards, under and over each bar, with even tension until the end is reached.

Finish off by taking the thread down into the end of one of the bars. Refer to diagrams.

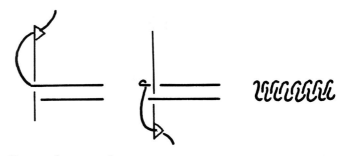

*Rectangular woven bars*

### Leaf-shaped woven bars

Leaf-shaped woven bars are worked in the same way as rectangular woven bars except that the two foundation bars are made using the same two holes. In addition the tension is controlled so that the two ends are pointed. This is achieved by pulling the first three or four weaving stitches firmly, loosening the tension for the stitches in the middle, then tightening the tension again for the last three or four stitches.

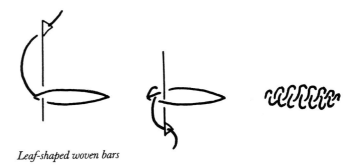

*Leaf-shaped woven bars*

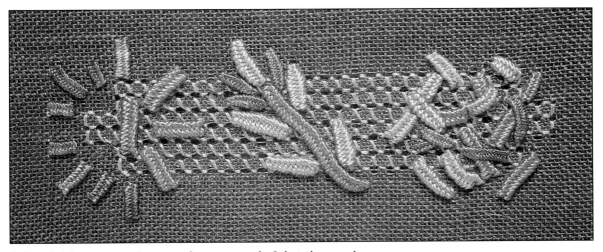

*Left and right—rectangular woven bars; centre—leaf shaped woven bars.*

## *Woven picots*

Woven picots may be long or short.

Belfast fabric colour 638 olive green
DMC coton perle no. 8:
    642 beige grey dark for four-sided stitch
    356 terracotta medium
    758 terracotta very light
    948 peach flesh very light
    950 sportsman flesh
    3041 antique violet medium
DMC coton perle no. 5 754 peach flesh light
Minnamurra coton perle no. 8 8130 mauve/
    violet

### *Short woven picot*

Insert a large-headed pin vertically into the fabric as shown at the top of the photograph. Bring needle and thread out approximately 3 mm (⅛") to the left of where the pin emerges from the fabric. Take the needle and thread around behind the head of the pin but not through the fabric, then into the fabric approximately 3 mm (⅛") to the right of the pin. The points where the thread enters and emerges from the fabric form the fixed base of the picot.

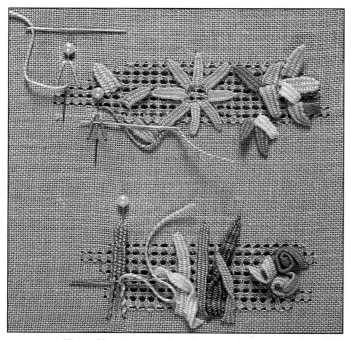

*Top—Short woven picot; bottom—long woven picot. The placement of the pins clearly shows the foundations and weaving. When the pin is removed only the base of the triangle is attached to the fabric.*

Bring the needle out at the point where the thread emerges from the fabric and back around behind the head of the pin again, not through the fabric, thus creating three foundation bars. Commencing at the head of the pin, weave from side to side, under and over the three foundation bars, not through the fabric, until the bars are completely covered. Finish off by taking the thread into the fabric at the base of the triangle. Remove the pin and the triangular picot will stand proud of the fabric, attached only at the base of the triangle. The picot may be manipulated into a petal shape and secured to the fabric with one stitch through its point.

### *Long woven picot*

Follow the instructions above for the short woven picot. In this case, however, the top of the pin is the detached point of the triangle and the base is stitched into the fabric for the required length, while the foundation bars are laid in the same manner as for the short woven picot. Start with a relatively long thread.

**Running out of thread**
Finish off the old thread by wrapping it around one of the foundation bars and securing the end in the fabric at the back of the work.

    Bring in a new thread by wrapping around one of the other foundation bars; restart the weaving.

## *Curl stitch, wrapping and overcasting*

Curl stitch and overcasting are traditional elements of Casalguidi embroidery. Four short curl stitches forming a diamond shape were often used to finish off the centre of a Venetian rosette (see page 37). It is easier to use a single thread or 6 undivided strands of stranded cotton as the wrapping thread rather than multiple lengths. Tight tension gives the best results.

Quaker fabric 610 sage
DMC stranded cotton 522 fern green for four-
    sided stitch background (2 strands)
DMC coton perle no. 5:
    754 peach flesh light
DMC coton perle no. 8:
    758 terracotta very light
    356 terracotta medium

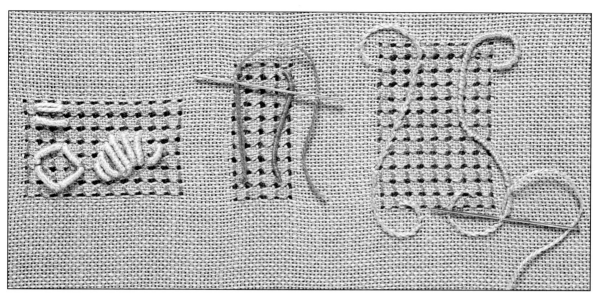

*Left—short curl stitch; centre—long curl stitch; right—overcasting*

### Short curl stitch

Stitch two firm foundation bars between two points 5 mm (¼") apart, bringing the needle and thread out at one end. Stitch around the two bars, wrapping above the surface of the fabric, i.e. not through the fabric. Firm tension assists in keeping this stitch evenly wrapped.

### Long curl stitch

Worked in the same way as a short curl stitch to form a straight wrapped bar between two points. To make a curved wrapped bar between two points make the tension of the two foundation bars quite loose, then lock them in place at one end with a firm buttonhole stitch. Wrap around the two foundation bars, holding the index finger of the other hand under them to allow better control of tension. (The two long stitches which remain at the back of the work may be secured on the back away from the hole of the four-sided stitch.) Stitch the wrapped bars in place with a fine matching sewing cotton or one strand of stranded cotton.

### Overcasting
(right-hand example in photo)

Work stem stitch on the design line then overcast or wrap around the stem stitches, not through the fabric, to create a smooth raised line. Make stem stitches even and take each overcasting or wrapping stitch around two stem stitches.

### Continuous wrapping

In traditional Casalguidi embroidery overcasting was used to create continuous smooth lines and scrolls. I find the technique of wrapping a core of yarn from a fixed point, then couching it to the design line, easier to manage than overcasting (follow the diagrams).

**Core** Using one or two long lengths of yarn in a tapestry needle, take the yarn into the back of the fabric and out to the front one or two fabric threads away. Adjust the yarn until the ends are all the same length. These threads form the core.

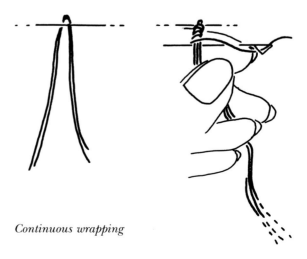

*Continuous wrapping*

**Wrapping thread** Attach a long single length of yarn to wrap around the core, bringing it out of the fabric from the same hole as the core. The wrapping thread must be approximately four times longer than the distance to be wrapped, long enough to finish the distance required without joining. (A new wrapping thread cannot be attached without first grounding the old wrapping thread into the fabric.)

The core yarn must be held taut while it is wrapped. A firm tension will result in smoother wrapping. Hold the core yarn in the left hand (right hand for left-handers) while you take needle and thread round and around the core, tensioning it on the index finger of the left hand (refer to diagram).

When wrapping is complete make a buttonhole stitch to lock it and prevent it from unravelling.

Couch the wrapping to the design line with a matching sewing cotton or single strand of stranded cotton. The couching stitch should be brought out on the design line, around the wrapped core and back through the same hole of the fabric to retain the smoothness of the line. The couching stitches must be close enough to hold the wrapping in place, i.e. approximately 5 mm (¼") apart. Take excess threads to the back and neatly stitch ends into existing work.

**Lock stitch** If you need to interrupt the wrapping of a long length of core yarn simply make a buttonhole stitch (half hitch) around the core with the wrapping thread. This is easily undone prior to resuming the wrapping.

### Ladder stitch

Ideal for joining two edges together without stitches showing.

# CEMBELLISHMENTS

## Hems

### Rolled hem

Narrow rolled hems approximately 6 mm (¼")
wide are a classic feature of Casalguidi
embroidery.

Allow 1.5 cm (⅝") from the hemstitching line
to the edge of the fabric. Count the number of
fabric threads between one edge and the hemstitching line and keep the number of threads
constant on all four sides.

After marking the hemstitching line with pins
withdraw the fabric thread along the line. First
snip it in the centre with small, sharp embroidery scissors, then, using a needle, withdraw the
thread a little at a time until the corner is
reached. Allow the withdrawn thread to hang
free until the hemstitching lines on the other
three sides have all been withdrawn, then cut
them off.

Fold the edge over approximately 4 mm (⅛"),
finger-press in place and fold it again to meet
the hemstitching line. Finger-press the second
fold.

Tack or baste the hem in position. Don't
mitre the corners but simply fold one side over
another.

To make flat tidy corners, trim a very small
amount of thread, equal to no more than one
thread width, off the end of the rolled hem with
sharp scissors.

Hemstitch in place, adding a couple of extra
stitches at each corner to hold the folds
together.

If the ends of the fabric threads have frayed
stitch the corner together with a fine crewel or
sharps needle and matching sewing cotton
before hemstitching.

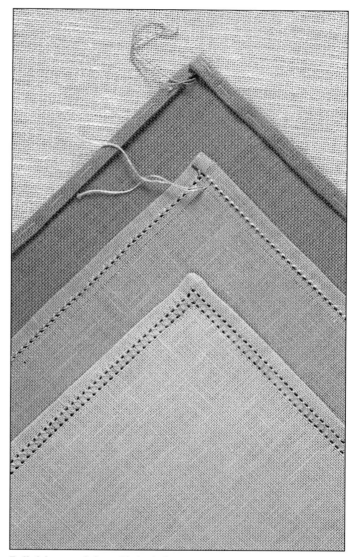

*Rolled hem and four-sided stitch:*
*1. Rolled hem showing corner fold and withdrawn thread*
*on hemstitching line.*
*2. Finished hemstitching and a withdrawn fabric thread*
*showing preparation for a row of modified four-sided*
*stitch adjoining the hemstitching.*
*3. Finished hemstitching and modified four-sided stitch.*

*Mitred corners and hemstitching:*
*1. Tack-marked fabric showing the cutting line and withdrawn thread on the hemstitching line.*
*2. Diagonal lines across the corners shown in relation to the cutting line (1), fold for hem (2), fold for edge (3) and hemstitching line (4).*
*3. Corner in process of cutting.*
*4. Mitred corner and hem tacked in place ready for hemstitching.*
*5. Finished hem.*

### Mitred corners

Mitred corners are suitable for hems wider than 6 mm (½"). Preparation is the key to a good result and time is well spent in preparing the edge and corners before hemstitching. Practice the process first on paper or a small piece of fabric to better understand it.

**Step 1** Create guidelines by counting fabric threads for accuracy and marking these lines with running stitches. Following the diagram:
*Line 1*: Cutting edge to remove excess fabric—withdraw one thread of fabric piece.
*Line 2*: Fold of seam allowance and edge of hem to be stitched to line 4, eight fabric threads inside line 1. The example in the photo shows the threads withdrawn, not run-stitched.
*Line 3*: Fold for edge of article.
*Line 4*: Hemstitching line—count ten threads in from line 3, withdraw one thread or mark with run-stitching.

**Step 2** Draw two diagonal pencil lines 6 mm (¼") across the corner as shown in the diagram and photograph and cut along the line closest to the corner.

Fold the material on the true bias at the corner point of the finished article.

Finger-press this fold firmly but do not stretch.

Turn the edge under, fold the seam allowances of the hems in place and slip stitch the edges of the mitred corner together.

Fold the hems and pin or tack in preparation for hemstitching.

Hemstitch using a matching or contrasting thread.

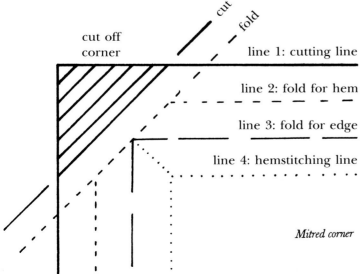

*Mitred corner*

## Hemstitching

Working on the back of the article, and following the diagram, start with a waste knot at A, 6 cm (2½") from B.

*Step 1:* Working from left to right, pick up 4 fabric threads with the needle as shown on the middle diagram, and take the needle and thread around a bunch of 4 fabric threads on the hemstitching line.

*Step 2:* Take the needle and thread through the fold of the hem 2 fabric threads away from the edge, from underneath it to the top at C, with firm tension. Repeat steps 1 and 2 until you reach a corner.

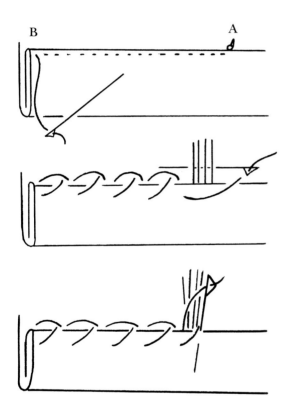

*Hemstitching*

At the corner you may end up with exactly 4 threads, but you are just as likely to have to pick up 2, 3 or 5 if the number of threads along the side is not evenly divisible by 4.

## Insertion stitches

Insertion stitches may seem a little daunting at first. It is often very helpful to practice them on scraps of linen before working the actual article. Such a sample will determine the thickness of thread required for the stitch and the distance between stitch units.

**Laced knotted buttonhole insertion** (left side of photo on next page)
Permin linen:
24 blue wing
78 autumn leaf
DMC coton perle no. 5:
932 antique blue dark
806 peacock blue dark

Hem the edges of the article with rolled hems (page 45).
1. Work knotted buttonhole stitches as shown in diagrams A, B and C on edges which are to be joined together in step 2. Stitches should be approximately 6 mm (¼") apart to create loops between the knots.
2. Lace two edges together with two overcasting stitches as shown in diagram C through loops made in step 1. The overcasting stitches are not worked through the fabric except to start and finish off.

**Decorative knotted stitch** (centre of photo on next page)
Permin linen:
78 autumn leaf
131 wild raspberry
DMC coton perle no.5:
209 lavender dark
tapestry needle size 24

This stitch is worked on the front of the article on either side of the seam.
Hem the edges with rolled hems (page 45).
Lay two edges side by side and join them together with ladder stitch (page 44).
Work steps 1 and 2 of the diagram on one side of the seam, alternating with steps 3 and 4 on the other side. Steps 2 and 4 are not worked through the fabric.

*Insertion stitches: left—laced knotted buttonhole; centre—decorative knotted; right and front—Italian.*

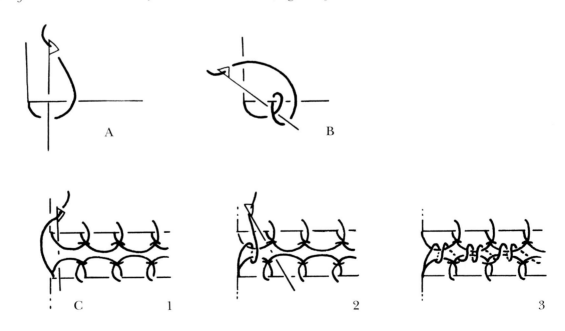

*Laced knotted buttonhole insertion*

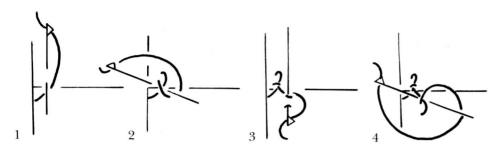

*Decorative knotted stitch*

**Italian insertion** (right side and front of photo)
Permin linen:
    131 wild raspberry
    76 prairie grain
DMC coton perle no. 8:
    471 avocado green very light
DMC coton perle no. 5:
    806 peacock blue dark
tapestry needle size 24

The edges of the two hems to be joined are kept 6 mm (¼") apart by first stitching them onto typing paper. Rule two pencil lines on the paper, pin and run-stitch the hems to the paper.

    Working from the top down, stitch onto both hems of fabric following the steps in the diagrams. The points where the needle enters the hem on each side are staggered or zigzagged, not kept opposite each other.

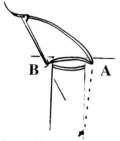

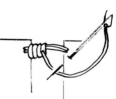

**1.** Using either perle 5 or perle 8 thread bring the needle and thread up through hem on the right hand edge, starting with a waste knot. Make two stitches between A-B.

**2.** Work 4 detached buttonhole stitches over B-A, from left to right, between the two fabric edges.

**3.** Make a buttonhole stitch on the right fabric edge, approximately 3 mm (⅛") below A and 2 fabric threads in from the edge.

Steps 1–3 complete the starting procedure.

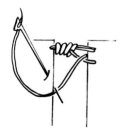
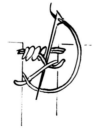

**4.** Make a buttonhole stitch on the left fabric edge approximately 5 mm (⅜") below the previous stitch on the left.

**5.** Make 4 detached buttonhole stitches around the buttonhole stitch previously made on the right fabric edge. The first stitch is worked in the centre of the space and the rest worked towards the right hand fabric edge.

**6.** Make a buttonhole stitch on the right edge approximately 5 mm (⅜") below the previous stitch on the right.

**7.** Make 4 detached buttonhole stitches around the buttonhole stitch previously made on the left fabric edge. The first stitch is worked in the centre of the space and the rest worked towards the left hand fabric edge.

Repeat steps 4–7 until complete. When thread runs out finish off and start through the hem in either step 4 or 6.

*Italian insertion stitch*

Another characteristic of Casalguidi embroidery is to finish off articles with tassels, bobbles, picots and buttonhole fastenings with loops.

# TASSELS AND PICOTS

## Tassels

### Basic tassel (see photo on next page)

Wind thread around a card pattern made of mat board or heavy card cut to the required tassel size. Tie the top with a double knot after passing a length of thread between tassel and card with a tapestry needle.

Remove the bunch of thread from the card by placing the card sideways on a table and pushing off the thread.

Tie the neck with a 40 cm (16") length of thread with an overhand knot, then flip the tassel over and tie another overhand knot on the other side and tighten. This knot, referred to as a double tie and wrap, is shown in the diagram.

Wrap the ends around the neck, taking each end of the ties behind the neck with a tapestry needle to blend them into the skirt of the tassel.

Leave the ends of the tassel uncut for a looped tassel, or cut and trim with a sharp pair of scissors.

The tassel is now complete.

### Tassel with mesh hood (see next page)

Make a basic tassel as described above. To make a mesh hood, buttonhole stitch above the neck of the tassel, beginning by taking a needle threaded with approximately 1.5 m (1½ yds) of yarn up through the skirt and out just above the tied neck.

With the head of the tassel held towards you make about 10 to 12 buttonhole stitches around the neck tie, evenly spaced and approximately 2 mm (¹⁄₁₀") apart. When you reach the first stitch again, stitch into it, and keep on stitching into the previous row, spiralling up to the holding cord. As the head curves in to the top, tighten the tension of your stitches. In the case of a large head you may need to decrease the number of stitches by working a stitch into every second stitch of the previous round (or as necessary).

Finish off the remaining thread by running it around the top row like a drawstring, then pull up the thread and take it down to blend with the skirt of the tassel.

### Running out of thread

Should your thread run out before you have finished buttonhole stitching the head of the tassel, leave the tail-end of the yarn hanging while you thread a new needle and yarn up through the skirt, bringing it out through the same hole as the tail of yarn. Continue with the new thread, going back later to finish off the tail-end by taking it down to blend in the skirt.

---

*Centre top and bottom right—two antique knotted tassels on foundations of linen fabric, stitched and trimmed with linen thread. Collection of the author.*
*Left—knotted tassels hang from a wrapped wooden bead. Knitting, rayon and suede ribbons as well as fancy knitting yarns and cotton perle threads make up this double knotted tassel.*
*Centre—rolled linen fabric forms the foundation of the head of this Italian style tassel buttonhole trimmed with multi-knotted tassels of DMC Cébélia crochet cotton no. 10.*
*Top right—the foundation for the head of this tassel is made from linen fabric. A linen cylinder 5 cm (2") long is made from a length of linen approximately 20 cm × 46 cm (8" × 18") or larger, following the instructions on page 58. Another length of linen 8 cm × 25 cm (3" × 10") reduced to 2 cm (¾") deep is wrapped and stitched around the centre of the first cylinder. The shape is buttonhole stitched all over and rows of buttonhole are attached to the fabric in the two concave corners. It is then decorated with single buttonhole bars. The tassel skirt is made from twelve plastic jug (pony) beads each covered with glue and wound with two 1 m (1 yd) lengths of yarn. The ends are knotted several times approximately 8 cm (3") from the beads and stitched into the bottom of the shape. A twisted cord and another covered plastic bead over-stitched with French knots are stitched to the top of the tassel.*

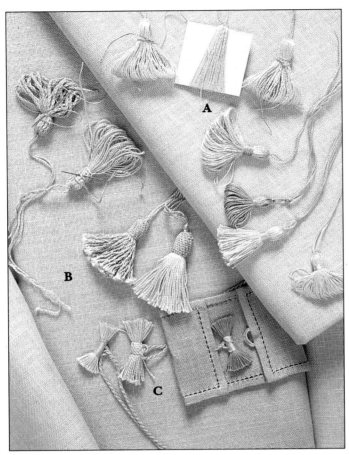

*A—basic tassel; B—tassel with mesh hood; C—button tassels.*

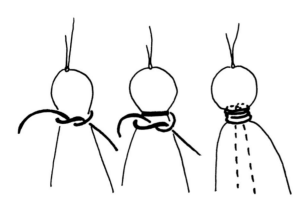

*Double tie and wrap*

## Button tassels

These delightful trimmings are often used with a loop to hold two openings together. A button tassel consists of threads wrapped around a hairpin crochet hook or a U-shaped hook cut from one end of a metal coathanger.

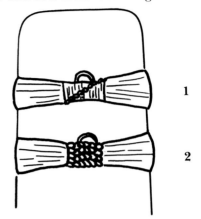

Wrap embroidery yarn around metal shape, 40 times for coton perle no. 8 and 30 times for stranded cotton or coton perle no. 5. Leave a tail of thread approximately 50 cm (18") long to add buttonhole stitch trim after the bunch has been secured.

Secure each bunch by stitching matching coloured sewing cotton with a sharps or crewel needle through the centre and around the bunch.

Buttonhole stitch the tail of embroidery yarn around the centre of the bunch, working horizontally along its length for approximately 6 mm (½"). As you work the buttonhole stitches allow the looped edge to roll around the bunch, as in 1 on diagram above. Finish off the thread by taking it back through the middle of the bunch.

Another way of decorating the button tassel is to buttonhole stitch around the bunch, holding it vertically, and spiralling around it in the same way as a mesh hood tassel (2 on diagram).

Make a loop in the middle of the button tassel by working buttonhole over two straight stitch bars approximately 6 mm (½") long, threading the tail of thread into the tassel.

Create a loop on the edge opposite the button tassel by working buttonhole stitch over two straight stitch bars approximately 6 mm (½") long, starting and finishing the thread in the hem of the article.

## Knotted tassels

Knotted tassels, used since the Renaissance on Italian cut-work and lace, are a characteristic of Casalguidi embroidery. Coton perle threads are most suitable for making these delightful trimmings.

### Single knotted tassels

1. Make knotted threads from single, double or triple lengths of yarn 1 m (1 yd) long. *Tie a single knot, leave a space of 2 cm (¾"), tie a single knot, leave a space of 6 mm (¼")*, repeat to end of yarn (refer diagram A below).

2. Make a string of knotted threads by piercing the yarn between the knots with a needle threaded with 50 cm (½ yd) yarn (refer diagram B below).

3. As they are strung onto the needle and yarn knots are tied onto this yarn, separating three or four knotted threads into groups to create texture and pattern. Refer diagram C below.

Cut and trim the yarn in the 6 mm (¼") spaces between the knots, indicated on the diagram by dotted lines. Finished strings resemble diagram D.

4. Variations may be made by attaching more knotted threads as shown in diagram E.

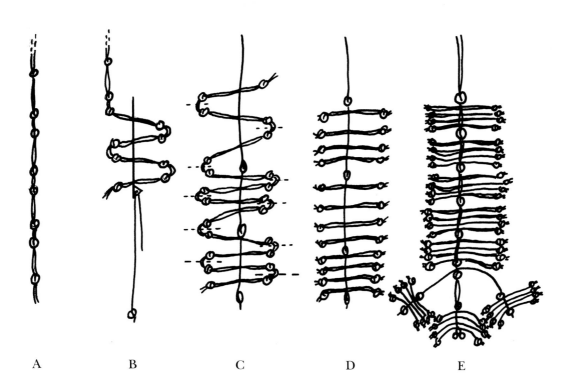

A   B   C   D   E

*Different types of knotted tassels*

*A—single, double and multi knotted tassels; B—tied bunches of knots; C—tied bundles of fabric threads; D—tied bunches of knots.*

### Double and multi-knotted tassels

These are made in the same way as single knotted tassels except that two or more knots are tied on top of each other at intervals.

### Tied bunches of knots

A variation of the above is to leave the loops uncut.

### Tied bundle of fabric threads

Left-over fabric threads may be stitched together in bundles with matching sewing cotton, then tied together with embroidery yarn, to form knotted strings as in the photograph above.

### Corner tassels

Cut a card pattern approximately 3 cm (1¹⁄₁₀") wide and position it over the corner of a rolled hem. Thread 1–2 m (1–2 yds) of yarn into a tapestry needle and double it. Wind the doubled yarn around the card pattern and through the corner of the hem. Refer to photo. Take the ends of the yarn into the hem to finish. Remove the card, tie the neck of the tassel against the edge of the hem and leave the skirt looped.

### Corner picots

Starting with approximately 2 cm (2¼ yds) of yarn make a soft buttonholed ring approximately 2 cm (¾") in diameter.

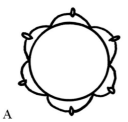

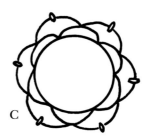

A                    B                    C

*Corner picots*

*Row 1:* Pin-mark the ring into six equal parts and make one loose buttonhole stitch at each division, removing the pins. This creates six loops around the buttonhole stitched ring (see A on diagram).

*Row 2:* On each loop work approximately 7 buttonhole stitches (or another uneven number) so that there is a middle stitch on which the picot is worked.

Make a picot on the middle stitch of each loop by working a bullion stitch with 3 to 5 wraps, with the needle pointing away from the circle as you wrap. Refer to B on diagram. Finish buttonhole stitching the rest of the loop. Work the other five loops in the same way.

*Variation:* Work row 2 without the picot, make a long loose buttonhole stitch between the centres of each buttonholed loop and work a third row with picots, adding more stitches to each loop (see C on diagram). Should a new thread be needed finish off the old thread and start the new one in the middle of the buttonholed ring.

## Buttonholed fastening loops with picots

Many traditional Casalguidi bags were finished with buttonholed loops at the top of the bag (with or without a picot in the centre of each loop). An interesting alternative to the traditional evenly sized loops is seen on the Barrier Reef bag on page 62.

Make loops on the top edge of the bag by working buttonhole stitch over two straight stitch bars approximately 12 mm (1") long, starting and finishing off the thread in the hem of the article. Add a picot in the middle of the loop by working a bullion stitch with three to five wraps, with the needle pointing away from the loop as you wrap. Refer to diagram for corner picots. Work each loop with the same number of buttonhole stitches.

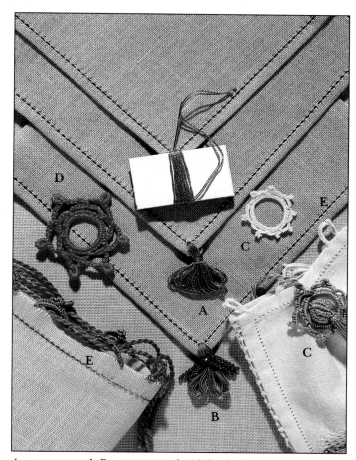

*A—corner tassel; B—corner tassel with beads; C—corner picot with one row of loops; D—corner picot with two rows of loops; E—buttonhole fastening loops with picot.*

# BOBBLES AND CORDS

## Bobbles

Bobbles are another distinctive feature of Casalguidi embroidery. They come in numerous different shapes and sizes, influenced largely by the nature of the foundation material. Don't throw away 'mistakes'—they can be easily disguised with bullion stitch or woven or buttonholed bars to become 'non-mistakes'.

Wooden beads, available in an endless variety of shapes and sizes, make excellent foundations. (A friendly woodturner might supply you with out-of-the ordinary shapes.) Wooden beads can be sprayed or brush painted, or covered with fabric and buttonhole mesh. Quilt wadding such as Pellon makes excellent soft foundation shapes. Self-coloured linen fabric is ideal for creating foundations to match a project; this method offers a number of unique shapes.

Most bobbles are covered with buttonhole stitching or a variation called Valsesian stitch, which creates the vertical 'bricking' pattern used to cover the bobbles on the antique Venetian rosette bag on page 74.

Buttonhole stitching may be started in two ways—with stitches attached to a soft foundation or with a ring of buttonhole stitches made separately and glued onto the wooden foundation.

Instructions are given for all these variations. I suggest that initially you use thicker thread such as coton perle no. 5 until you are familiar with the process.

### Starting buttonhole stitch on bobbles with wooden or other hard foundations

Make a small buttonholed ring around a special embroidery tool called a ring stick or the cut end of a skewer stick.

Using approximately 1.5 m (1½ yds) of thread in a tapestry needle, wrap the end of the thread two or three times around the smallest diameter of the ring stick, anti-clockwise if working the buttonhole stitch from left to right, clockwise if working

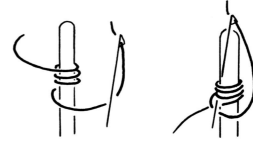

stitching right to left. Work a minimum of 8 buttonhole stitches around the ring stick.

Take the buttonholed ring off the stick, apply a small amount of colourless fabric adhesive to the top of a wooden bead and glue the buttonholed ring to it. Allow 5–10 minutes drying time. Continue buttonhole stitching; depending on the size of the bead, start increasing in the second round by working two stitches into every second stitch of the previous round. Continue stitching, increasing as necessary to cover the fullest part of the bead. As the bead becomes smaller decrease by working in the alternate stitches of the previous round until the bead is covered. As it takes quite a few metres of thread to cover the average bead you will have to finish off old threads as you work and bring in new strands.

Leaving the tail of the old thread to hang, bring in a new thread by taking the needle and thread through the same hole as the old thread, again leaving a tail hanging, and continue stitching for a few rounds.

Re-thread the tails in a tapestry needle and take them back through the same hole and out at the bottom of the bead.

Glue the tails to the bottom of the bead and cut off excess.

*Increasing and decreasing buttonhole stitches*
To increase, work two stitches into every second stitch of the previous round. In the next round work one stitch in every stitch of the previous round. Repeat this as necessary.

To decrease work one stitch into every second stitch of the previous round, or as necessary to maintain even spacing.

### Starting buttonhole stitch on bobbles with soft foundations

Thread a tapestry needle with approximately 1.5 m (1½ yds) of thread, and knot the end. Take the needle and thread from the bottom to the top of the soft foundation, e.g. wadding or linen. Make 2 straight stitches 6 mm (½") long to create foundation bars and work 4 buttonhole stitches on one side; turn the bobble around and work 4 buttonhole stitches on the other side between the first 4 stitches.

*Starting the buttonhole stitch*

Continue working buttonhole stitch; depending on the size of the bead, start increasing stitches in the second round by working two stitches into every second stitch of the previous row. Continue stitching, increasing as necessary to cover the fullest part of the bead. As the bead becomes smaller decrease by working one stitch in alternate stitches of the previous row, continuing until the bead is covered. As it takes quite a few metres of thread to cover an average bead you will have to finish off old threads as you work and bring in new strands, following the instructions given above. Finish off the loose tails by re-threading them in a tapestry needle and taking them back through the same hole, stitching into the foundation and cutting off excess.

### Soft fabric foundation around a pencil or stick

Cut soft cotton or gauzy fabric into long strips approximately 2 cm (¾") wide. Wrap the strips

A—buttonhole stitch over a wooden bead foundation.
B—buttonhole stitch over a soft foundation.
C—wooden bead with linen fabric.
D—bobble made on a linen foundation.
E—gathered edge of a linen foundation cylinder.
F—buttonhole stitch on a linen foundation cylinder.
G—soft fabric around a pencil or stick.
H—quilt wadding foundation.

around a pencil, folding the fabric in almost every round to build up the centre of the 'bead'.

Stabilise the roll by stitching vertical wraps of sewing cotton around the fabric, and remove it from the needle. It is now ready to be covered with buttonhole stitch. Refer to photo.

### Quilt wadding foundation

Soft bobbles can also be made with Pellon. Cut a strip of Pellon 2.5 cm (1") wide. Fold and roll it very tightly until it forms a ball and stitch into place. Refer to photo.

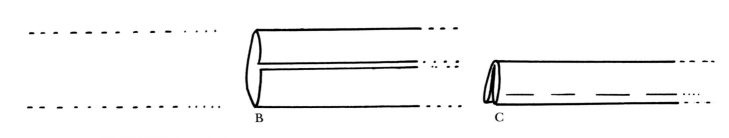

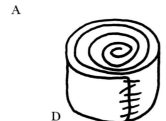

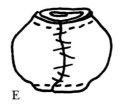

*Making a bobble on a linen foundation cylinder*

### Valsesian stitch

Starting on either a soft or hard foundation in the manner described above, stitch around the bobble following the diagram for Valsesian stitch, which is worked from left to right. This

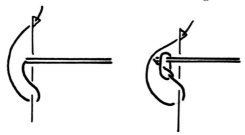

stitch is best worked in a thick corded thread such as Cébélia crochet cotton or coton perle nos. 3 or 5.

### Wooden bead with linen fabric

A wooden bead may be covered with linen fabric by folding the fabric around the shape and stitching it in place with matching coloured sewing cotton or by gathering a circle of fabric around the bead. Refer to photograph.

### Bobble made on linen foundation cylinder

When using coloured linen for a project you may wish to make bobble foundations in the same linen.

Cut a long strip of fabric four times the width of the final length of the bobble and 12 cm (5") or more long. Fold the fabric lengthwise so the

long edges meet in the middle, and press. Fold again so the two edges are aligned and press again. Run-stitch the edges together to make the next step easier. (Diagrams A–C.)

Roll the fabric once tightly around a skewer stick or pencil, stitching to hold fabric in place. Keep on rolling until you have reached the desired size, cut off excess fabric and stitch the end down. Remove pencil. Stitch back and forth through the rolled fabric to prevent it slipping out of shape. (Diagram D.)

This shape when buttonholed gives a cylindrical form with the top and bottom edges forming sharp angles. If you want soft curved edges gather the fabric before covering it with buttonhole stitches. Thread a needle with 2 strands of sewing cotton and run-stitch around each end of the cylinder, pulling firmly to gather and draw in the edge. (Diagram E.)

Working the buttonhole stitch over a cylindrical roll of fabric is quite a different matter to working a gently rounded bobble. Start in the same way as buttonhole stitching around a soft foundation (on previous page), threading a crewel needle with approximately 1.5 m (1½ yds) of yarn knotted at the end. Take the needle and thread up through the linen and bring it out at the top of the shape. Make two straight stitch foundation bars 12 mm (½") long and work 4 buttonhole stitches on one side; turn the bobble around and work 4 buttonhole stitches on the other side between the first 4 stitches.

*Buttonhole stitch over a cylindrical roll of fabric*

Continue, stitching through the fabric as you work each stitch, increasing in the second and subsequent rounds by working 2 stitches into every second stitch in the previous round, working towards the edge of the cylindrical shape and keeping the stitches evenly spaced.

*Important:* It is easier to work this part of the bobble using a crewel or chenille needle, picking up the fabric with each stitch. The last round in which you are picking up the fabric is right on the edge. At this point change to a tapestry needle and continue down the shape, *not* stitching through the fabric, until the whole shape is covered, decreasing stitches in the last few rounds. To decrease at the bottom, work one stitch into every second stitch of the previous round, or as necessary to maintain even spacing.

As it takes quite a few metres (yards) of thread to cover the bobble you will have to finish off old threads and bring in new strands, following the directions given above and cutting off the excess tails.

## Buttonholed rings

Buttonholed rings are stitched around a pencil or ring stick in the same way you start buttonhole stitch for a bobble with a wooden or hard foundation. Refer to the diagram on page 56. The difference with buttonholed rings is that the stitches are worked firmly and close together. The last stitch is taken into the first stitch from underneath. Finish off the thread by overcasting 3 or 4 stitches in the loops of the previous stitches. Cut off excess thread.

### Chained rings

Each ring of a chain of rings is worked separately. Make one buttonholed ring as above, and hold it against the pencil or ring stick while you start a new ring, taking the foundation wraps through the ring as well as around the pencil. Continue adding rings to make chains. Two or more rings may be worked in a single ring. The bag on page 70 is heavily decorated with chained rings.

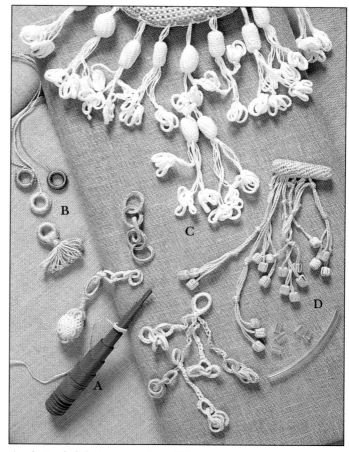

A—*buttonholed ring on a ring stick.*
B—*buttonhole stitched plastic curtain rings.*
C—*chained rings.*
D—*plastic tubing available at hardware stores is sliced with a Stanley knife and wrapped with thread to make unusual tassels.*

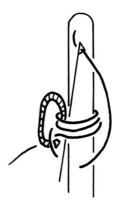

*Chained rings*

59

## *Wrapped beads and plastic tubing*

Milk jug or pony beads with large holes or short pieces of plastic tubing make foundations which can be wrapped with thread. Cut 2 m (2¼ yds) yarn and tie it through the bead at its centre-point with a double knot, slipping the knot into the hole. Using a tapestry needle, stitch one tail of the thread around the bead, through the hole; when the first tail of thread runs out use the other tail. Finish off the ends inside the bead.

# *Cords*

Any of these cords may be used as finishing touches.

## *Four-strand round braid*

Two steps repeated make this plaited braid which is pinned to a soft board or tied to a hook during working. To make the cord thicker use doubled or tripled (or more) lengths of yarn for each strand. Referring to the diagram repeat the two steps:

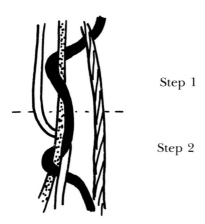

Step 1

Step 2

**1.** Take the outside right thread behind the next two threads to lie between the third and fourth threads on the left.
**2.** Take the outside left thread behind the next two threads to lie between the third and fourth threads on the right.
Repeat to the end, twisting and tightening the cord as you work.

## *Hand-made twisted cords*

A general rule of thumb when measuring thread to make a cord is to take four times the length of the required cord. You may need a helper for longer cords but if you don't have one hook the yarn around a wardrobe key or door knob and place a chair at the halfway point to stabilise the coiled yarn.

Double the yarn by hooking it over the door knob or door key. Twist the doubled cord together between thumb and index finger until it is tightly coiled. Holding the end in one hand, double the cord and hold it taut with the other hand at the halfway point. Let it twist back on itself and tie an overhand knot at the end to prevent unravelling.

## *Machine-made twisted cords*

Twisted cords can be made very quickly using a sewing machine, utilising the bobbin winder situated on the top of some machines. You also need the kind of bobbin which has holes in it. If you don't have a machine with a top-winding bobbin with holes, you can use masking tape to attach the ends of the cord to the outer part of the machine's flywheel and follow the same procedure (outlined below).

Most threads and yarns are suitable for machine twisting. Experiment with different weights and thicknesses to achieve the result you want.

A very attractive cord is made by twisting together 3, 4 or more lengths of 6-stranded cotton.

A general rule of thumb when measuring the thread for a machine-twisted cord is to take approximately three times the required finished length.

Tie the thread through a hole in the bobbin or attach it with masking tape to the flywheel of the sewing machine. Hold the cord at a right angle to the winder, using the other hand to create a loop with thumb and forefinger around the cord, near the bobbin, thus forming a channel to keep the thread from winding around the bobbin. Hold the thread slightly slack to allow for the twisting which will shrink the length of the cord. If you hold the cord too tightly you may pull the bobbin off the machine.

You will know the cord is twisted enough when little 'curls' appear in the thread near the bobbin.

Find the midway point with your other hand and fold the cord in two, keeping it taut to prevent uneven twisting. Hold the first 2.5 cm (1") of the folded end of the cord and allow it to twist. Move fingers along the cord for another few centimetres (inches) and let that portion twist. Allow the rest of the cord to twist gradually.

Cut the thread off the bobbin and tie all the ends together with an overhand knot.

Finish off the knotted end by stitching or creating a tassel.

Longer cords may be hooked around a wardrobe key or doorknob and a chair placed halfway to stabilise the coiled yarn. When twisting longer cords you may need to add extra twists by hand on the end away from the machine, in the same direction that the cord twists, as there are more twists closer to the bobbin than a greater distance away.

### Finishing off the knotted end

*By stitching*

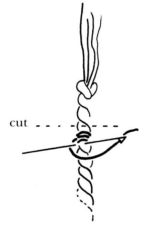

cut

Trim the knotted end by first stitching through the cord securely with a sharps needle threaded with matching sewing cotton. Wind the sewing thread around the cord 4 or 5 times, stitching through the cord again and cutting off the unwanted end, including the knot.

*By creating a tassel*

Make a card pattern the desired length of the tassel.

Thread a tapestry needle with two or three 1 m (1 yd) lengths of yarn.

Position the knot of the cord at the top of the card and wrap the thread around the card, pushing the needle through the knot with each wrap.

Remove the bundle of threads from the card, tie the neck and trim the skirt.

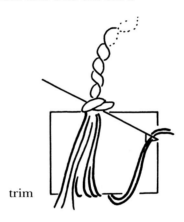

trim

For more details about making decorative tassels and cords refer to my *Decorative Tassels and Cords*, also published by Kangaroo Press (1995).

# The Projects

Innovative designs were inspired by the art of the Near East, the Far East, Africa and South America.

## Embroidery guide and stitch code

Before you begin a project I recommend you prepare and identify the threads.

1. Copy the key for the project and keep it with the threads.

2. Set aside all the threads for a project in a special container.

3. Tag each thread with the stitch code assigned to it in the key. Alternatively, punch holes in a piece of light cardboard, write the colour number and code letter beside each hole; cut off a number of pieces 50–100 cm (18"–36") long, and attach them to the appropriate hole.

A letter of the alphabet on its own (e.g. C) signifies the stitch to be used, its thread and colour.

A letter of the alphabet with a number after it (e.g. C2) also signifies the stitch to be used, its thread and colour. The number is used where the same stitch is to be worked in a different thread and/or colour.

| | |
|---|---|
| **A** | modified four-sided stitch |
| **B** | padded raised stem band |
| **C** | bullion stitch |
| **D** | wrapping |
| **E** | buttonhole stitch triangles |
| **F** | curl |
| **G** | single buttonhole bars |
| **H** | double buttonhole bars |
| **I** | Venetian rosette |
| **J** | raised stem unpadded |
| **K** | satin stitch padding |
| **L** | buttonhole stitch space filler |
| **M** | woven picots |
| **N** | woven bars |
| **O** | straight stitch |
| **P** | double buttonhole bars with 1 extra row |
| **Q** | 4-sided stitch on withdrawn threads |
| **R** | French knots |
| **S** | running stitch |
| **T** | double buttonhole bars with 2 extra rows |
| **U** | corner picot |

PAGES 62–63 *Barrier Reef Bag. Colourful four-sided stitch background on an uneven grid of withdrawn threads, bullion, wrapping and buttonhole stitches. The eyes of the fish are shaped with single buttonhole bars using DMC coton perle no. 12. Knotted tassels are made from perle thread, stranded cotton, knitting ribbon and strips of suede. Effie Mitrofanis.*

# 1 TRADITIONAL MOTIFS

Four characteristic traditional designs are given in this section, each with design diagram, list of materials and stitches used. Embroider the motif as it is on the article of your choice, enlarge or reduce it in size, repeat the design to make central motifs, corners and borders—go back to pages 6–19 for historical reference, forward for modern interpretations.

## Bullions, bars and wrapping

### Materials

Belfast fabric colour 101 antique white
DMC coton perle no. 8: ecru (background)
DMC Cébélia crochet yarn no. 10: white
tapestry needle size 24
milliner's needle size 1 or crewel needle size 3

### Instructions

Transfer the rectangular background shape and work this area first in modified four-sided stitch.

Transfer the shapes of the surface stitches and work them following the key.

| Key | Stitch | Page | Thread | Details |
|-----|--------|------|--------|---------|
| A | mod. 4-sided | 30 | perle 8/ecru | |
| B | padded raised stem band | 39 | Cébélia/white | |
| C1 | bullion, 10 wraps | 38 | Cébélia/white | double yarn |
| C2 | bullion, 15 wraps | 38 | Cébélia/white | |
| C3 | bullion, 10 wraps | 38 | Cébélia/white | single yarn |
| D | wrapping | 42 | Cébélia/white | |

*TRADITIONAL MOTIFS*

# *Octagonal motif*

## *Materials*
Belfast fabric colour 101 antique white
DMC coton perle no. 8: white (background)
DMC coton perle no. 12: ecru
DMC coton perle no. 8: ecru
Tapestry needle size 24
Milliner's needle size 1 or crewel needle size 5

## Instructions
Transfer the square background shape and
work this first.

Transfer the shape of the surface stitches and
work them following the key.

## Special instructions
The core of the padding is made from 20
lengths of coton perle no. 8 (10 lengths
doubled); the satin stitch is worked in the same
thread.

Raised stem band is worked in coton perle
no. 12.

The first row of the two buttonhole stitch triangles has 14 stitches.

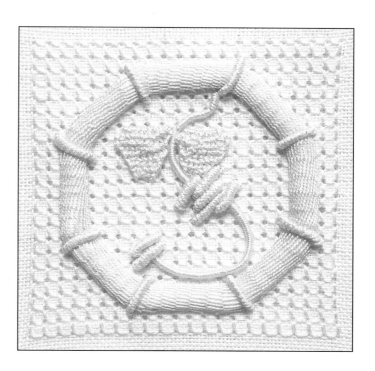

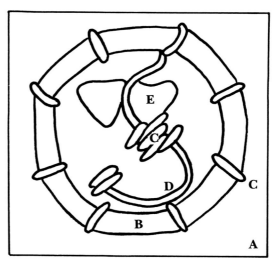

| Key | Stitch | Page | Thread | Details |
|-----|--------|------|--------|---------|
| A | mod. 4-sided | 30 | perle 8/white | |
| B | padded raised stem | 39 | perle 12/ecru | |
| C | bullion | 38 | perle 12/ecru | 16 wraps, 3 strands yarn |
| D | wrapping | 42 | perle 12/ecru | Core: 10 strands |
| E | buttonhole stitch triangles | 36 | perle 8/ecru | Row 1: 14 stitches |

# Dragon

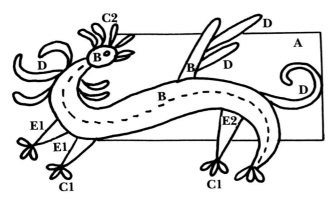

*Materials*

Belfast fabric colour 101 antique white

Linen thread size 30/2 white (approximately equal to no. 8 perle)

DMC coton perle no. 8 white (background)

tapestry needle size 24

milliner's needle size 1 or crewel needle size 3

## Instructions

Transfer the background shape and work this first.

Transfer the shape of the surface stitches and work them following the key.

## Special instructions

Padding for raised stem band for the body of the dragon (see page 39 for detailed instructions) is made by laying, side by side, two rows of padding each with a core of 20 strands of coton perle no. 8 (10 strands doubled). Where the body narrows at each end, cut strands of yarn from the cores, tapering the padding to fit the shape. Cover the padding with single satin stitches (worked over the two cores together). Stitch the foundation bars over the padding and work the raised stem band, adding rows where necessary to fill the shape.

The two front legs of the dragon are buttonhole stitch triangles shaped as follows:
*Row 1:* 6 buttonhole stitches; *row 2:* 5 stitches; *row 3:* 4 stitches; *row 4:* 3 stitches; *row 5:* 2 stitches; *row 6:* 1 stitch; *row 7:* 1 stitch.

The dragon's back leg is made as follows:
*Row 1:* 8 buttonhole stitches; *row 2:* 7 stitches; *row 3:* 6 stitches; *row 4:* 5 stitches; *row 5:* 4 stitches; *row 6:* 3 stitches; *row 7:* 2 stitches; *row 8:* 1 stitch; *row 9:* 1 stitch.

The dragon's eye is a French knot.

| Key | Stitch | Page | Thread | Details |
|---|---|---|---|---|
| A | mod. 4-sided | 30 | perle 8/white | |
| B | padded raised stem | 39 | linen | |
| C1 | bullion, 10 wraps | 38 | linen | Feet |
| C2 | bullion, 12 wraps | 38 | linen | Head |
| D | wrapping | 42 | linen | Core: 10 lengths |
| E1 | buttonhole stitch triangles | 36 | linen | Row 1: 6 buttonhole st* |
| E2 | buttonhole stitch triangles | 36 | linen | Row 1: 8 buttonhole st* |

*add one extra stitch at the end of the triangle

## *Trifoil (three-petalled) flower, bar, bullions and wrapping*

*Materials*
Belfast fabric colour 101 antique white
DMC coton perle no. 8 ecru
tapestry needle size 24
milliner's needle size 1 or crewel needle size 3

**Instructions**
Transfer the background shape (inside the bullion bars) and work this area first.

Transfer the shapes of the surface stitches and work them following the key.

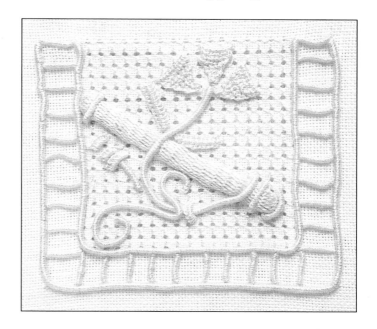

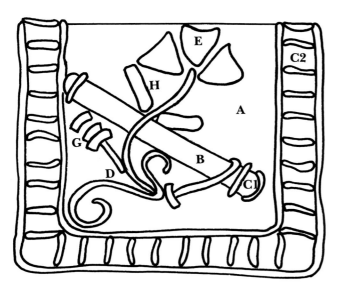

| Key | Stitch | Page | Thread | Details |
|-----|--------|------|--------|---------|
| A | mod. 4-sided | 30 | perle 8/ecru | |
| B | padded raised stem | 39 | perle 8/ecru | |
| C1 | bullion, 24 wraps | 38 | perle 8/ecru | |
| C2 | bullion, 20 wraps | 38 | perle 8/ecru | |
| D | wrapping | 42 | perle 8/ecru | Core: 6 lengths |
| E | buttonhole stitch triangles | 36 | perle 8/ecru | Row 1: 10 stitches |
| G | single buttonhole bars | 33 | perle 8/ecru | |
| H | double buttonhole bars | 34 | perle 8/ecru | |

# 2 Pouches and Purses

Depending on the subject being embroidered secondary stitching could be varied by using bullion stitch to interpret fruit and grapes and single and double buttonhole bars for leaves.

*Mythical creatures such as the gryphon were often a source of inspiration.*

# *Venetian rosette purse with picot and tassels*

This delightful little purse is embroidered with
a traditional Venetian rosette, bullion stitches,
wrapped threads and buttonholed bars. The
sides are joined with Italian insertion stitch.

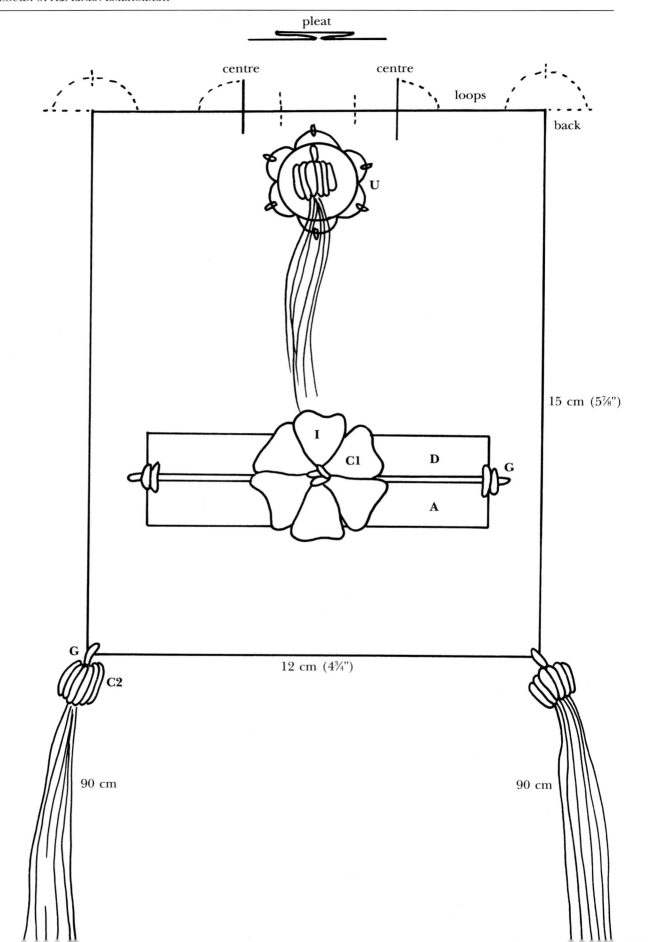

pleat

centre          centre

loops

back

U

15 cm (5⅞")

I

C1

D

G

A

G

12 cm (4¾")

G

C2

90 cm          90 cm

*Materials*

30 cm × 70 cm (16" × 20") Belfast fabric colour
   233 antique ivory
1 ball coton perle no. 8 ecru (background)
1 ball coton perle no. 8 927 grey-green light
3 small plastic jug or pony beads
tapestry needle size 24
milliner's needle size 1 or crewel needle size 3

*Finished size* 15 cm × 12 cm (5⅞" × 4¾")

## Instructions

Tack-mark the pattern to the fabric with sewing
cotton allowing 8 cm (3") all around for hems
and handling.

Transfer the rectangular shape and work this
first.

Transfer the surface stitches and work them
following the key.

## Special instructions

All surface embroidery is worked in coton perle
no. 8, 927.

The first row of the buttonhole stitch triangles of the Venetian rosette contains 14 stitches.

## Making up and finishing

Finish the edges of the front and back of the
bag with rolled hems (see page 45). Join sides
and base with Italian insertion stitch in coton
perle no. 8 ecru.

Fold a small pleat in centre front and centre
back of the top edge of the bag and stitch in
place. Make a corner picot and stitch it to the
centre front top edge.

Make three tassels using the beads as bases.
Make the bobbles first, working vertical bullion
stitches around each bead and finishing
through the hole, in perle no. 8 927. Leave 8
cm (3") tails of thread hanging from each completed thread and stitch more threads into the
bottom of each bobble until you have approximately 16 threads to form the skirt.

Attach a tassel over the corner picot and to
each corner of the base of the bag.

Make buttonhole loops with picot (page 55)
at the top of the bag as shown on the diagram
and in the photo.

Make a twisted cord from four 2 m (2 yd)
lengths of perle no. 8 ecru. Thread it in and out
through the buttonhole loops twice around the
top of the bag and stitch the two ends together.

| Key | Stitch | Page | Thread | Details |
|---|---|---|---|---|
| A | mod. 4-sided | 30 | perle 8/ecru | |
| C1 | bullion, 8 wraps | 38 | perle 8/927 | |
| C2 | bullion, 12 wraps | 38 | perle 8/927 | 2 lengths yarn |
| D | wrapping | 42 | perle 8/927 | Core, 6 lengths |
| G | single buttonhole bars | 33 | perle 8/927 | |
| I | Venetian rosette | 37 | perle 8/927 | Row 1: 14 stitches |
| U | corner picot | 54 | perle 8/927 | |

## Antique Venetian rosette bag

This Venetian rosette bag is a copy of an antique. The materials I have listed are the closest available today. This bag, with its combination of embroidery and bobbles, is one of the most popular classic examples of Casalguidi embroidery.

*Materials*
35 cm × 70 cm (12" × 24") Belfast fabric colour
   101 antique white or colour 233 antique ivory
Linen thread or DMC coton perle no. 8 ecru
tapestry needle size 24
milliner's needle size 1 or crewel needle size 3

*Finished size* Approximately 51 cm × 19 cm (20¼" × 7½")

**Instructions**
Tack-mark the pattern to the fabric with sewing cotton allowing 8 cm (3") all around for hems and handling.

Transfer the rectangular background shape and work this first.

Transfer the surface stitches and work them following the key.

**Making up and finishing**
Stitch a rolled hem around all four edges (see page 45).

Fold 16.5 cm (6½") of the length of the fabric to create a pocket and join the sides with Italian insertion stitch.

Seven pairs of bobbles are made from rolled linen foundations covered in Valsesian stitch (see pages 57 and 58). The larger bobbles are 12 mm (½") and the smaller bobbles 10 mm (⅜") in diameter.

| Key | Stitch | Page | Thread | Details |
|-----|--------|------|--------|---------|
| A | mod. 4-sided | 30 | All stitches in | |
| B | padded raised stem | 39 | perle 8/ecru | |
| C | bullion, 8 wraps | 38 | or linen | |
| D | wrapping | 42 | | Core: 6–8 lengths |
| F | curl | 42 | | |
| G | single buttonhole bars | 33 | | |
| I | Venetian rosette | 37 | | |

# Scrolling beads pouch with beaded tassel

*Finished size* 7 cm × 8 cm (2¾" × 3⅛")

**Instructions**

Tack-mark the front and back of the bag to the centres of the fabrics with sewing cotton to allow fabric all around for hems and handling.

Transfer the rectangular background shape and work this first.

Sew the sapphire feature bead in place.

Transfer the shapes of the surface stitches and work them following the key.

Sew the antique blue heather beads on with waxed sewing cotton, stitching twice through each bead to hold it securely.

**Making up and finishing**

Stitch a rolled hem around all four sides of both pieces of fabric. Join the bottom and sides with Italian knotted insertion stitch in coton perle no. 8 colour 312. Add a beaded tassel.

**Beaded tassel**

Thread beading needle with 1 m (1 yd) sewing cotton, fold double, pull through beeswax and tie a knot at the end to prevent the beads falling off.

Make the centre of the tassel by following the line on the diagram for step 1 between A and B and threading 41 beads onto the cotton.

Add another 8 beads, shown solid on the diagram, and take the needle and thread through bead C to form a loop of beads. Repeat this step making 3 more loops through D, E and F, and finish the thread through the beads above F.

Cut the threads off the needle and knot the ends together. Thread another 1 m (1 yd) sewing cotton as above and following the dotted line on the diagram for step 2 create a row of beads down the left side of the tassel centre.

Make 3 pendants to hang from the central bead at the base of the tassel as shown in the diagram for step 3. Pendant a with 8 beads, counting the turn-around bead, is made on the left side of the central bead, pendant b, also with 8 beads, is on the right and pendant c with 12 beads is on the left.

Take the needle and thread back through the central bead and continue up the other side.

Stitch the ends of the threads through a jug

*Materials*

20 cm (7") square Permin linen 06524 colour blue wing (front)

20 cm (7") square Permin linen 065131 colour wild raspberry (back)

DMC stranded cotton, 1 skein each:
    3768 grey green dark (background)
    824 blue very dark
    3809 turquoise dark

1 ball DMC coton perle no. 8 312 navy blue light

2 plastic jug (pony) beads

Mill Hill antique beads 03013 blue heather

Mill Hill Glass Treasures 12043 sapphire (feature bead)

sewing cotton, violet          beading needle
tapestry needle size 24      beeswax

(pony) bead wrapped with perle 8 colour 312 and attach the tassel to the centre of the base of the pouch.

Make a twisted cord from four 2 m (2 yd) lengths of perle 8 colour 312, fold it in half and attach it to the top of the bag at one side. Pull one end through the wrapped bead; tie a knot below the bead, leaving a 6 cm (2½") long tassel of 8 threads.

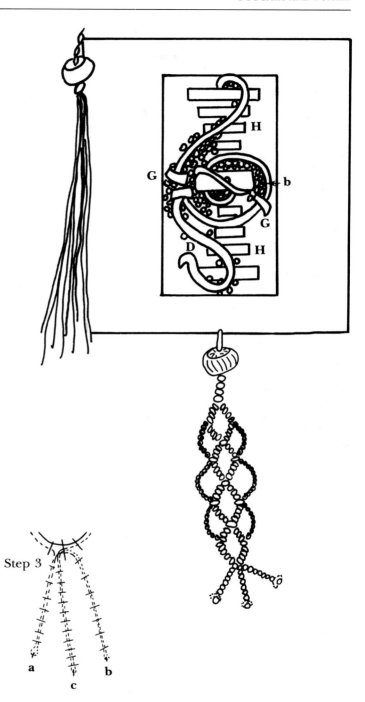

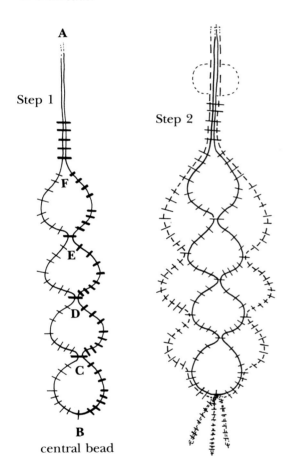

*Beading pattern for scrolling beads pouch*

| Key | Stitch | Page | Thread | Details |
|-----|--------|------|--------|---------|
| A | mod. 4-sided | 30 | 2 strands/3768 | |
| D | wrapping | 42 | 6 strands/3809 | Core: 12 strands |
| G | single buttonhole bars | 33 | 6 strands/3809 | |
| H | double buttonhole bars | 34 | perle 8/824 | |
| b | beading | | sewing cotton | |

## Pouch with seaweed tassel

*Finished size* 8 cm (3¼") square

**Instructions**

Tack-mark the front and back of the bag to the centres of the fabrics with sewing cotton to allow fabric all around for hems and handling.

This design has no background panel of four-sided stitch.

Transfer the shapes of the surface stitches and work them following the key.

**Special instructions**

The 3 buttonhole stitched triangles are made in gold yarn on top of 3 of the 6 petals of the Venetian rosette. To prevent unravelling, seal the ends of the gold yarn with fabric or craft glue before starting to embroider. Three or four single buttonhole stitches are worked at the end of each gold triangle to taper it.

**Making up and finishing**

Stitch a rolled hem all around (see page 45). Join sides and base with Italian insertion stitch. Fold two small pleats to the sides of the front of the bag and one pleat in the centre of the back and stitch them in place.

Make two buttonholed rings (page 59) and attach them to the top corners of the bag.

Make two multi-stranded cords to go through the rings, using 6 × 60 cm (24") lengths of coton perle no. 8 colour 782 for each one. Thread the 6 strands through each ring, double them and tie an overhand knot approximately 2 cm (¾") above the ring. Tie the ends of the two cords together with an overhand knot, forming a tassel approximately 4 cm (1½") long.

For the seaweed tassel, make two sets of chained rings (page 59), each of three rings chained through one ring, using coton perle

*Materials*

2 × 20 cm (8") squares Permin linen 065 colour 78 autumn leaf
DMC coton perle no. 8 782 topaz dark
Leah coton perle no. 5 531 violet
DMC *Fil or clair* gold yarn
Mill Hill antique glass beads colour 03029 autumn green
small gold and bronze coloured beads
tapestry needle size 24
beading needle
beeswax

| Key | Stitch | Page | Thread | Details |
|-----|--------|------|--------|---------|
| E | buttonhole stitch triangles | 36 | *Fil or clair* | 3 triangles<br>Row 1: 14 stitches* |
| G | single buttonhole bars | 33 | *Fil or clair* | |
| I | Venetian rosette | 37 | perle 8/831 | 6 triangles<br>Row 1: 15 stitches |
| | beads | | sewing cotton | centre of rosette |

* add three or more single stitches to taper off the end of the triangles

no. 8 colour 782. Finish off the tails of the rings by stitching them all through one point of the last ring so they form a fixed group. Tie an overhand knot in the threads coming from each bunch of rings, then tie two overhand knots in the combined threads and take the tails two at a time into the hem to finish off.

Make a seaweed tassel with 4 beaded pendants following the design pattern. Each pendant is made using a strand of waxed cotton folded double in the needle with a knot on the end to prevent the beads falling off. Position the beads in the middle of the thread leaving two long tails at the top to attach the pendant to the bag.

Each pendant of beads with side sprays is made by first threading approximately 48 beads from A to B as shown in the diagram. Leave the last bead as the turn-around and thread the needle back 4 beads to C. Thread another 6 beads, turn around the last one and re-thread them back to the main stem to create a side spray D-C. Make another side spray from the same point C and thread the needle back through 3 beads of the main stem to E and make 2 more side sprays. Repeat this procedure until all side sprays are complete. There are approximately 3 beads between E and F and 11 between F and G. Thread back through the rest of the beads to A to complete the pendant.

Stitch the pendants through the knots of the chained rings and finish the ends in the hem of the bag.

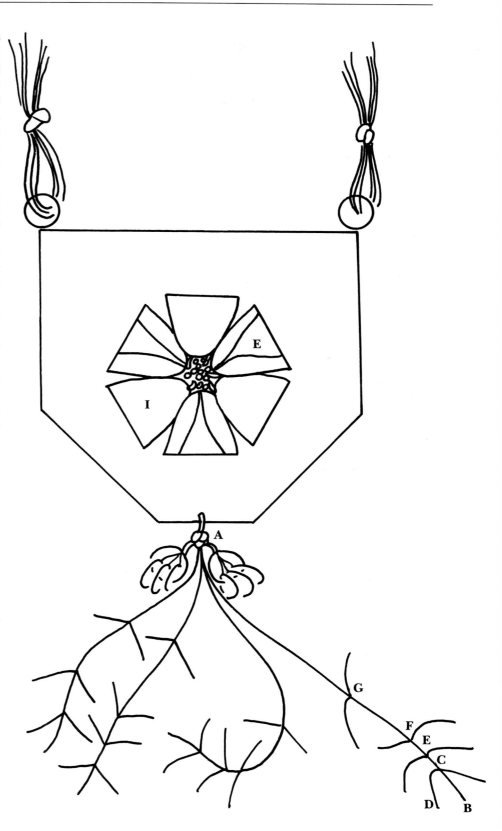

# 3 Designs for Cushions, Bags and Panels

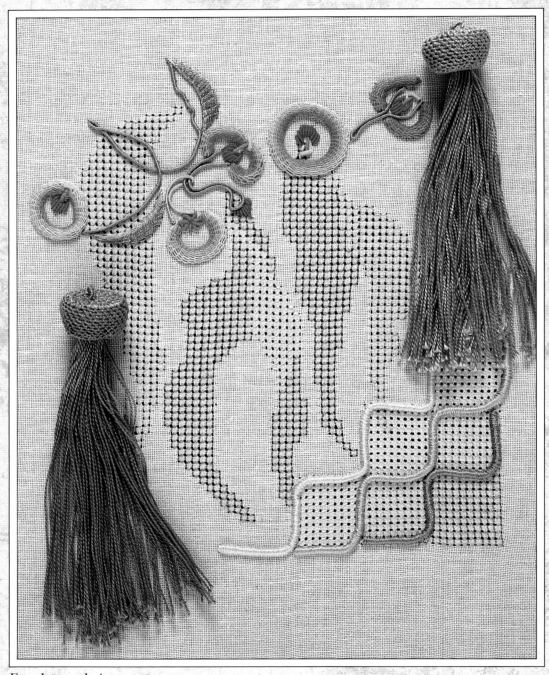

*Eucalyptus design*

# Eucalyptus design

This eucalyptus design may be used on a cushion cover or any type of household linen. Parts of the design could be extracted to be used on any article you choose.

*Materials*

50 cm (½ yd) Quaker fabric colour 718 silver (actually a pale grey green)

DMC coton perle no. 8, 1 ball each:

931 antique blue medium
932 antique blue light
3752 antique blue very light
926 grey green medium
927 grey green light
928 grey green very light
309 rose deep
335 rose
498 Christmas red dark
899 rose medium
776 pink medium

DMC coton perle no. 5, 1 skein each:

931 antique blue medium
932 antique blue light (tassels)

1 skein DMC stranded cotton colour 3820 yellow ochre

tapestry needle size 24

milliner's needle size 1 or crewel needle size 3

## Instructions

Transfer the irregular leaf shapes and the stepped shape at bottom right for the background and work these areas first.

Transfer the shapes of the surface stitches and work them following the key.

## Special instructions

*Circles of pink flowers* These flowers, numbered 1–5, are worked in padded raised stem band in the colours indicated in the key. Pad the areas with satin stitched raised padding (see page 39), using 20 lengths of coton perle no. 8 in a matching colour. Work satin stitch over the padding and make the foundation bars for the raised stem band with the same colour.

*Raised stem band worked in a circle* Work raised stem band stitch starting at the outer edge of the circle and spiralling in towards the centre.

To conceal the point where the colour changes remove the needle from the working thread and let it hang, and thread the new colour in the needle. After attaching the new thread to the back of the work, bring it to the surface near one edge of the circle, behind previous raised stem stitches, and out through the same hole as the previous working thread. Work the new colour for a while, then thread the hanging tail of the old colour into another needle and take it to the back of the work, pulling it lightly so as not to create a dent in the surface of the stitching.

*Flower centres in bullion stitch* All bullion stitches are made by wrapping 12 times around the needle, except for the yellow bullions in flowers 4 and 5 worked in colour 3820 yellow ochre which are worked with 6 strands of stranded cotton wrapped 8 times around the needle.

**Decorative tassels**

Make two decorative tassels on a bobble base, in coton perle no. 5 colours 931 and 932, using the methods shown on pages 51 and 58. Make a bobble by rolling a piece of linen fabric, approximately 4 cm × 30 cm (1½" × 12") into a cylinder, giving a finished size approximately 3 cm (1") in diameter.

Work buttonhole stitches in coton perle no. 5 to cover the bobble. Make a skirt for the tassel by wrapping coton perle no. 5 in the same colour 50 times around a card template 15 cm (6") long. Tie the top of the tassel with yarn approximately 1 m (1 yd) long; stitch the remaining yarn through the centre of the finished bobble. Make a buttonholed loop at the top of the bobble and stitch it to the embroidery. Cut and trim the skirt.

*Diagram and key on following pages.*

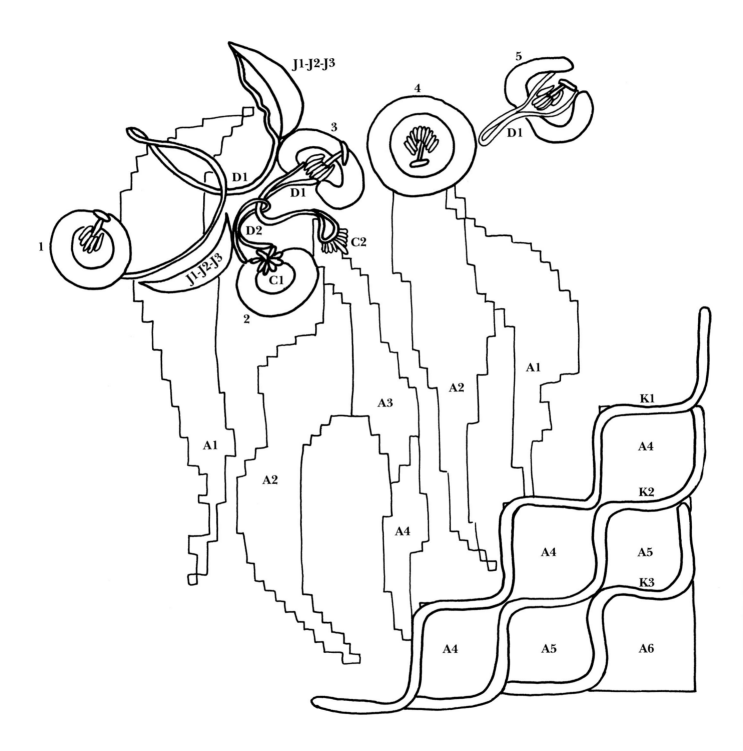

| Key | Stitch | Page | Thread | Details |
|-----|--------|------|--------|---------|
| A1<br>A2<br>A3<br>A4<br>A5<br>A6 } | mod. 4-sided | 30 | perle 8/932<br>perle 8/931<br>perle 8/3752<br>perle 8/928<br>perle 8/927<br>perle 8/926 | |
| B1<br>B2<br>B3<br>B4<br>B5 } | padded raised<br>stem band | 39 | perle 8/776<br>perle 8/899<br>perle 8/309<br>perle 8/335<br>perle 8/498 | |
| C1<br>C2<br>C3<br>C4<br>C5 } | bullion | 38 | perle 8/309<br>perle 8/498<br><br>perle 8/498<br>perle 8/335<br>3 strands/3820 | 12 wraps<br>1 lge: 10 wraps<br>8 sml: 8 wraps<br>Centres: 12 wraps<br>Pistil: 12 wraps<br>Ends: 8 wraps |
| D1<br>D2 | wrapping<br>wrapping | 42 | perle 8/926<br>perle 8/927 | |
| J1<br>J2<br>J3 } | raised stem<br>unpadded | 40 | perle 8/309<br>perle 8/927<br>perle 8/926 | midrib of leaf<br>middle of leaf<br>edge of leaf |
| K1<br>K2<br>K3 } | satin stitched<br>padding | 39 | perle 8/928<br>perle 8/927<br>perle 8/926 | |

**FLOWERS**

Flower 1: B1: 5 rows outer edge
    B2: 2 rows
    B3: 3 rows centre of circle
Flower 2: B1: 3 rows outer edge
    B2: 3 rows
    B3: 3 rows centre of circle
Flower 3: B2: 4 rows outer edge
    B4: 1 row
    B3: 3 rows centre of circle
Flower 4: B1: 3 rows outer edge
    B2: 2 rows
    B4: 2 rows
    B3: 3 rows centre of circle
Flower 5: B4: 5 rows outer edge
    B5: 2 rows centre of circle

**CENTRES OF FLOWERS 1, 3, 4 and 5**
C3 centre
C4 pistil
C5 ends

## Butterfly window and fabric tassel

This butterfly window design may be interpreted as a picture or translated onto any article you wish. The fabric tassel pattern may be used with other embroidery designs.

*Materials*
30 cm × 50 cm (12" × 18") Dublin fabric colour 774 blue violet
1 ball DMC coton perle no. 8 341 blue violet light
DMC coton perle no. 5, 1 skein each:
  792 cornflower blue dark
  939 navy blue
DMC stranded cotton, 1 skein each:
  3809 turquoise dark
  597 turquoise
  333 blue violet
  798 delft dark
  917 plum medium
  783 topaz
1 reel DMC *Fil or clair* gold yarn

tapestry needle size 24
milliner's needle size 1 or crewel needle size 3

### Instructions
Tack-mark the pattern to the fabric with sewing cotton allowing 8 cm (3") all around for hems and handling.

Transfer the rectangular background shapes and work them first.

Transfer the shapes of the surface stitches and work them following the key.

### Special instructions
Begin by outlining the top wings of each butterfly with back stitch in coton perle no. 5 colour 939. Work buttonhole stitch in coton perle no. 5 colour 792, not through fabric, in horizontal rows from the top of the wing downwards, catching the end of each row with a buttonhole stitch through a back stitch at each side. Refer to page 34 for more detailed instructions.

The two lower wings are worked in bullion stitches in 6 strands of stranded cotton with 14 wraps around a size 3 crewel or milliner's needle. The butterflies' feelers are made with two lines of running stitch, one line in DMC *Fil or clair* gold yarn and the other in one strand of stranded cotton colour 798. Seal the ends of the gold yarn with a little fabric glue to prevent fraying.

### Butterfly tassel

*Finished size* 11 cm × 6.5 cm (4½" × 2½")
Tack-mark the pattern to the fabric, allowing 8 cm (3") all around for hems and handling.

Work the background area first and embroider the butterfly following the key.

Finish three sides of the embroidered fabric with rolled hems and hemstitch (see page 45).

Turn the seam allowance at the top edge of the tassel and stitch. Attach a looped twisted cord to the seam allowance at the back and stitch the two ends of the seam allowance together to form a cylinder. Stitch three lines of running stitches above the line marked 'neck' on the pattern, using a doubled thread of sewing cotton. Pull each gathering thread firmly to create the 'head' of the tassel and stitch the edges together.

If desired work buttonhole stitch over the head to create a mesh.

*See next page
for tassel
pattern
and key
to stitches*

*Butterfly window pattern*

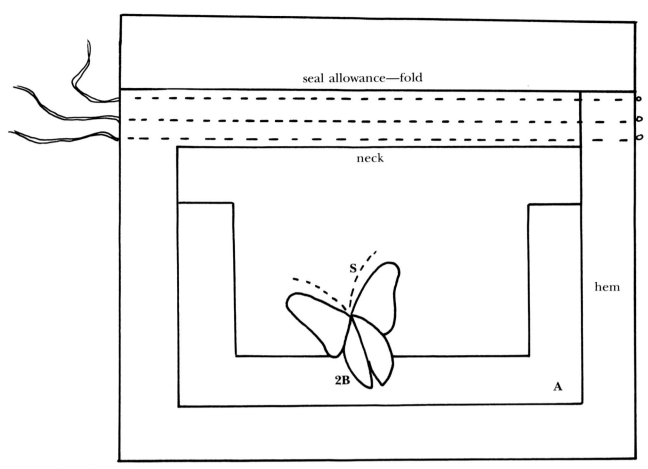

*Butterfly tassel pattern*

| Key | Stitch | Page | Thread | Details |
|---|---|---|---|---|
| **Background** | | | | |
| A | mod. 4-sided | 30 | perle 8/341 | |
| **All butterflies' top wings** | | | | |
| L | buttonhole stitch space filler | 34 | perle 5/939 perle 5/792 | back stitch outline buttonhole stitch |
| S | running stitch | | *Fil or clair* 1 strand/798 | feelers |
| **Butterflies' lower wings** | | | | |
| 1B | bullion 14 wraps | | 6 strands/3809 6 strands/597 | |
| 2B | bullion 14 wraps | | 6 strands/333 6 strands/917 | |
| 3B | bullion 14 wraps | 38 | 6 strands/333 6 strands 798 6 strands/3809 | |
| 4B | bullion 14 wraps | | 6 strands/333 6 strands/3809 6 strands/597 | |
| 5B | bullion 14 wraps | | 6 strands/333 6 strands/798 | |
| 6B | bullion 14 | | 6 strands/333 6 strands/917 6 strands/783 | |

## *Painted squares*

*Materials*

30 cm × 25 cm (12" × 10") Dublin fabric colour white

fabric paints: blue, turquoise blue, green and gold

household sponge

1 skein DMC stranded cotton 597 turquoise

DMC coton perle no. 8, 1 ball each:
   312 navy blue light
   806 peacock blue light

tapestry needle size 24

*Finished size* of painted square 15 cm × 18 cm (6" × 7")

### Background

Create a painted background with a sponge, fabric paints and brush. Cut out a 3 cm (1⅛") square of household sponge.

Apply paint to the sponge with an artist's brush and sponge on colours alternately to make a background approximately 15 cm × 18 cm (6" × 7"), leaving a border of plain fabric. Use the colours listed above or your own choice. Sponge gold paint lightly over every alternate square. Allow the paint to dry and fix it according to the manufacturer's instructions.

With one strand of stranded cotton colour 597 work four-sided stitch on alternate squares, following the irregular shapes made by the paint.

### Button tassels

Make 9 tied-thread button tassels following the instructions on page 52, using colour number 806 for the body of the tassels and colours 312 and 517 for the buttonhole stitch wrapping.

Use this painted and stitched fabric panel as the centre feature of a bag or cushion and trim with button tassels.

# Twilight Field

Twilight Field is a softly textured landscape worked on a misty blue Belfast linen. This design could be adapted to almost any article.

*Materials*
30 cm × 50 cm (12" × 18") Belfast fabric colour 594 misty blue
DMC coton perle no. 8, 1 ball each:
    340 blue violet medium
    926 grey green medium
    931 antique blue medium
    758 terracotta very light (or 1 skein stranded cotton)
    356 terracotta medium (or 1 skein stranded cotton)
DMC stranded cotton, 1 skein each:
    3809 turquoise green light
    3810 turquoise green medium

824 blue very dark
3807 lavender
tapestry needle size 24
milliner's needle size 1 or crewel needle size 3

**Instructions**
Transfer the irregular background shape and work this first.
    Transfer the shapes of the surface stitches and work them following the key.

**Special instructions**
Start at the top of the design with the straight stitches and work downwards.
    Each petal of the flowers in the foreground (M1 and M2) is made with woven picot stitch, manipulated to the required shape and stitched in place through the point of the picot.

## Tassels

*Bobbles*
931 antique blue medium

*Tassel 1*
931 antique blue medium
758 terracotta very light
356 terracotta medium

*Tassel 2*
340 blue violet medium
3809 turquoise green light
3810 turquoise green medium

There may not be enough thread left to make the tassels when the embroidery work is completed. The colours are the same ones used in the embroidery.

The double knotted tassels are attached to bobbles made on a fabric foundation (see pages 53 and 58). Make the buttonhole stitches covering the bobbles using 2 lengths of coton perle no. 8 colour 931 in the needle. Make the knots on the tassels from the colours listed.

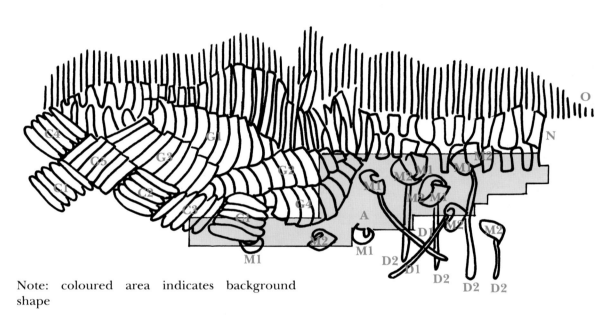

Note: coloured area indicates background shape

| Key | Stitch | Page | Thread | Details |
|---|---|---|---|---|
| A | mod. 4-sided | 30 | perle 8/931 | |
| C1 | | | 6 strands/3809 | |
| C2 | bullion | 38 | 6 strands/3810 | all 18-22 wraps |
| C3 | | | 6 strands/824 | |
| C4 | | | 6 strands/3807 | |
| D1 | wrapping | 42 | perle 8/340 | Core: 2 lengths |
| D2 | wrapping | 42 | 6 strands/3807 | Core: 6 strands |
| G1 | | | 6 strands/3809 | |
| G2 | single buttonhole bars | 33 | 6 strands/3810 | |
| G3 | | | 6 strands/824 | |
| G4 | | | 6 strands/3807 | |
| G5 | | | perle 8/340 | |
| M1 | woven picot | 42 | perle 8/758 | |
| M2 | woven picot | 42 | perle 8/356 | |
| N | woven bars | 41 | perle 8/926 | single bar foundations |
| O | straight | | perle 8/340 | |

# 4 HOUSEHOLD LINEN

The most sought after articles were items for intimate and domestic use.

*Casalguidi rose table-linen setting with plate and cutlery*

# *Table cloth, place mat, serviette and serviette ring*

The Casalguidi rose design is used here on table linen; it may be interpreted in different ways on other articles.

*Materials*

1 m (1 yd) Dublin fabric colour 322 fawn 140 cm (55") wide
1 skein DMC stranded cotton 725 topaz
DMC coton perle no. 8, 1 ball each:
    498 Christmas red dark
    816 garnet
    326 rose very deep
DMC coton perle no. 8, 2 balls:
    3041 antique violet
    sewing cotton to match fabric
    tapestry needles sizes 24 and 26
    crewel needle size 3
    milliner's needle size 1

Follow the cutting plan for the most economical use of fabric to make one of each article:
1. Table cloth 80 cm (31½") square
2. Serviette 45 cm (18") square
3. Place mat 50 cm × 40 cm (20" × 16")
4. Serviette ring 25 cm × 12.5 cm (10" × 5")

*Finished sizes* (approximate)
Table cloth 70 cm (27½") square
Serviette 40.5 cm (16") square
Place mat 44 cm × 34 cm (17½" × 13½")
Serviette ring 17 cm × 4 cm (6¾" × 1¾")

## Instructions

Transfer the rectangular shapes and work these areas first.

Transfer the shapes of the surface stitches and work them following the key.

The design diagram shows the complete design used on the corner of the table cloth.

The serviette design is a section of the corner of the tablecloth.

The place mat uses one side of the design with an extra three-petalled rose.

The serviette ring contains three narrow strips of four-sided stitch with a three-petalled rose in the centre.

## Special instructions

Embroider the roses by first stitching the centres (C) with 5 bullion knots in yellow stranded cotton colour 725 to form a triangle. Four of the bullion stitches are wrapped 10 times and one has 6 wraps.

Work the buttonhole stitch triangles for the petals following the design diagram and the key.

## Making up and finishing

Finish off the edges with rolled hems, or mitred corners and hem stitch, using coton perle no. 8 colour 3041.

Add generous tassels, choosing one of the styles from pages 51–54.

For a decorative touch, pin to the table cloth a tassel made from double knots hanging from a soft bobble buttonhole stitched with two lengths of coton perle no. 8 colour 326. Three groups of three knotted tassels made from colour 3041 are attached around the bobble. Another group of three long knotted tassels hang from the bottom of the bobble. Each group is made from colours 498, 816 and 326. All the knots are made from three lengths of yarn tied together.

*Diagram and key to stitches over page*

91

| Key | Stitch | Page | Thread | Details |
|-----|--------|------|--------|---------|
| A | mod. 4-sided stitch | 30 | perle 8/3041 | |
| C | bullion | 38 | 6 strands/725 | 4 bullions, 10 wraps each |
| | | | | 1 bullion, 6 wraps |
| E1 | | | perle 8/498 | Row 1: 10 buttonhole st * |
| E2 | buttonhole stitch triangles | 36 | perle 8/326 | Row 1: 8 buttonhole st * |
| E3 | | | perle 8/816 | Row 1: 12 buttonhole st * |

* add one extra stitch at the end of a petal to make it more pointed

serviette

table mat—add extra 3-petalled rose

# *Floral spray quilt squares*

These quilt squares may be made into any size project—cushion, quilt top, bedcover, runner, tablecloth, pillow sham. You need not embroider each square, but each one should be finished with a rolled hem and joined with Italian insertion stitch.

Squares of different coloured fabrics may be mixed in the patchwork tradition.

*Materials*

Belfast fabric colour 233 antique ivory (you will need a piece approximately 30 cm [12"] square for each quilt square)
DMC coton perle no. 8 ecru (background)
Needle Necessities overdyed coton perle no. 8:
  colour 848 pale violet/pink
  colour 817 pale apricot
tapestry needle size 24

*Finished size* 20.5 cm (8") square

## Instructions

Transfer the background shape in the centre of the square and work this area first.

Transfer the shapes of the surface stitches and work them following the key.

## Making up and finishing

Finish the edges with a rolled hem stitched with coton perle no. 8 ecru (see page 45).

Join the squares with Italian insertion stitch.

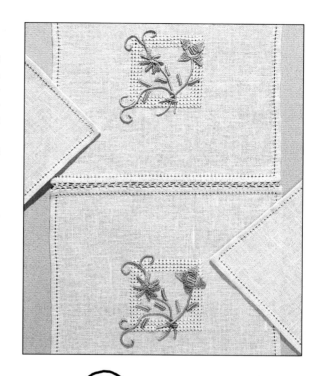

| Key | Stitch | Page | Thread |
|---|---|---|---|
| A | mod. 4-sided | 30 | perle 8/ecru |
| C | bullion 12 wraps | 38 | |
| D | wrapping (2 lengths for core) | 42 | |
| E | buttonhole stitch triangles | 36 | |
| G | single buttonhole bars | 33 | perle 8/848 or 817 |
| H | double buttonhole bars | 34 | |
| P | double buttonhole bars/ extra row | 34 | |

# Scrolls and flowers pillow sham

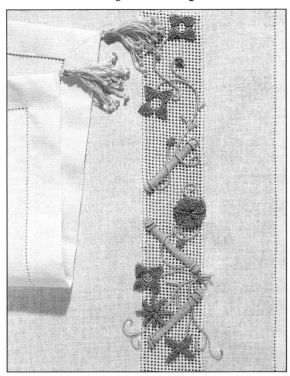

This design is also ideal for the ends of a table runner. The dimensions are easily changed.

*Materials*
1 m × 70 cm (40" × 27½") Belfast fabric colour
  222 cream
DMC coton perle no. 8, 2 balls:
  colour 739 tan ultra very light (background)
DMC coton perle no. 5, 2 skeins:
  colour 503 blue green medium
Minnamurra coton perle no. 8, 2 skeins:
  colour 8180 yellow/green

tapestry needle size 24
milliner's needle size 1 or crewel needle size 3

*Finished size* 75 cm × 48 cm (29½" × 19")

**Instructions**
Tack-mark the finished size of the pillow, allowing 10 cm (4") all around for hems and handling.

Transfer the background shape, positioning it parallel to a short side of the rectangle and approximately 10 cm (4") in from the edge of the finished size, centred between the two long sides. Work this area first on withdrawn threads (see page 29).

Transfer the shapes of the surface stitches and work them following the key.

**Making up and finishing**
Finish the edges with mitred corners 3.5 cm (1⅜") wide, hemstitched with coton perle no. 8 ecru. See page 45.

**Tassels**
Make 4 knotted tassels from coton perle no. 8 colour 739 (see page 53). Each tassel consists of 10 strings of knotted threads. Each string is made from 4 lengths of yarn with a finished length of 12 cm (5") between multiple knots tied 4 or 5 times. Bunch the 10 strings together and tie them around the middle with a double knot using a thread approximately 30 cm (12") long. Tie around the neck with a piece of yarn 1.5 m (1½ yds) long, leaving a short 5 cm (2") tail at one end.

With the long tail of thread make 11 button-

| Key | Stitch | Page | Thread | Details |
|-----|--------|------|--------|---------|
| Q | 4-sided stitch on withdrawn threads | 30 | perle 8/739 | |
| B | padded raised stem | 39 | perle 8/8180 | Padding 739 |
| C | bullion 12 wraps | 38 | perle 8/8180 | |
| D | wrapping | 42 | perle 8/8180 | Core: 4 lengths 739 |
| E | buttonhole stitch triangles | 36 | perle 5/503 | Row 1: 10 stitches |
| G | single buttonhole bars | 33 | perle 5/503 | |
| H | double buttonhole bars | 34 | perle 8/8180 | |
| I | Venetian rosette | 37 | perle 5/503 | Row 1: 11 stitches |
| P | double buttonhole bars/extra row | 34 | perle 5/503 | |
| T | double buttonhole bars with two extra rows | 34 | perle 5/503 | |

hole stitches around the neck, then, holding the tassel with the top towards you, buttonhole stitch around the head.

Make a single buttonhole bar at the top of the head to form a loop.

Stitch loose ends into the head of the tassel.

Decorate the tassel head with 8 bullion stitches, each 8 wraps around the needle, with colour 8180.

Stitch the tassels to the corners.

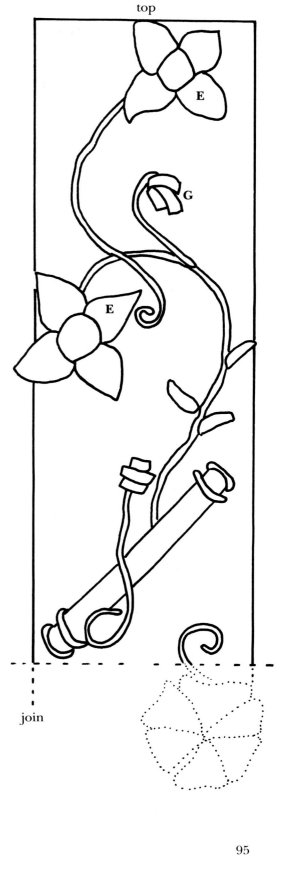

## Cornflowers tissue-box cover

The cornflowers tissue-box cover is made up of two components—a decorative top and a cover for the box. The decorative top is made of two rectangles of fabric, one embroidered and the other plain. Each rectangle is hemmed on all four sides and the long sides are joined together with Italian insertion stitch, leaving a gap in the middle of the join for the tissues to be pulled through.

The box cover is made separately with no base.

The decorative top is attached to the box cover with two Velcro dots for easy laundering and pressing.

The pattern given is for a medium size box holding 200 tissues.

*Materials*
40 cm × 140 cm (16" × 55") Dublin fabric
    colour 474 light plum
DMC coton perle no. 8, 1 ball:
    3041 antique violet (background)
DMC coton perle no. 5, 1 skein:
    792 cornflower blue dark
DMC coton perle no. 8, 1 ball each (or coton
    perle no. 5, 1 skein each):
    340 blue violet medium
    341 blue violet light
DMC stranded cotton, 1 skein each:
    310 black
    437 tan light
2 Velcro circles
narrow elastic
tapestry needle size 24

*Finished size*
Decorative top—27 cm × 30 cm (10⅝" × 11¾") including 1 cm (⅜") allowed for insertion stitch join.

**Preparing the pattern, laying and cutting the fabric**
Make paper patterns to include seam allowance of 5 cm (2") all around for each section of the decorative top and 2 cm (¾") all around for each part of the box cover, identifying each piece clearly.

Pin the pattern pieces onto the fabric following the cutting plan and cut them out. Leave the two parts of the decorative top (1/1) in one piece until the embroidery is complete, then cut.

**Instructions for embroidery**
Zig-zag stitch or overlock around the edge of the decorative top (1/1) to prevent fraying.

Tack-mark the shapes of the two rectangles onto the fabric.

Transfer the rectangular background shape to the centre of one of the above and work this area first.

Transfer the shapes of the surface stitches and work them following the key.

Work woven picots (M1–M3) attached to the fabric at the inner circle with their points positioned on the outer circle. The first round of woven picots may be attached to the fabric at their points by a small stitch. On three of the flowers a second layer of woven picots is worked on top of the first round in another colour.

French knots fill the centres after the woven picots have been completed.

**Making up and finishing the decorative top**
Cut the decorative top in half as indicated on the pattern.

Finish the edges of both rectangles with rolled hems and hemstitch with coton perle no. 8 colour 340. Work a row of modified four-sided stitch next to the hemstitch (see page 30).

Join two long sides of the rectangles with Italian insertion stitch (see page 49), leaving an 11 cm (4¼") opening for the tissues to be pulled through.

Attach the Velcro circles near the openings of the box cover and the decorative top to hold the two together.

**Making up the box cover**
To make the opening for the tissues place pattern pieces 3 and 4 on top of each other and machine stitch a rectangle approximately 11 cm × 8 mm (4¼" × ⅜") in the centre as shown on the pattern. Cut the fabric in the centre of the rectangle, cutting small nicks in the corners to prevent puckering after the next step.

Push one of the pieces of fabric through the opening made above so that the stitching is between the two layers, and press.

The top of the box cover is now ready for the sides of the box cover to be joined to it. Pin and tack one long edge of pattern piece 2 to the top of the box cover and machine stitch to within approximately 4 cm (1½") of the short ends. Pin the two short ends in place and machine stitch,

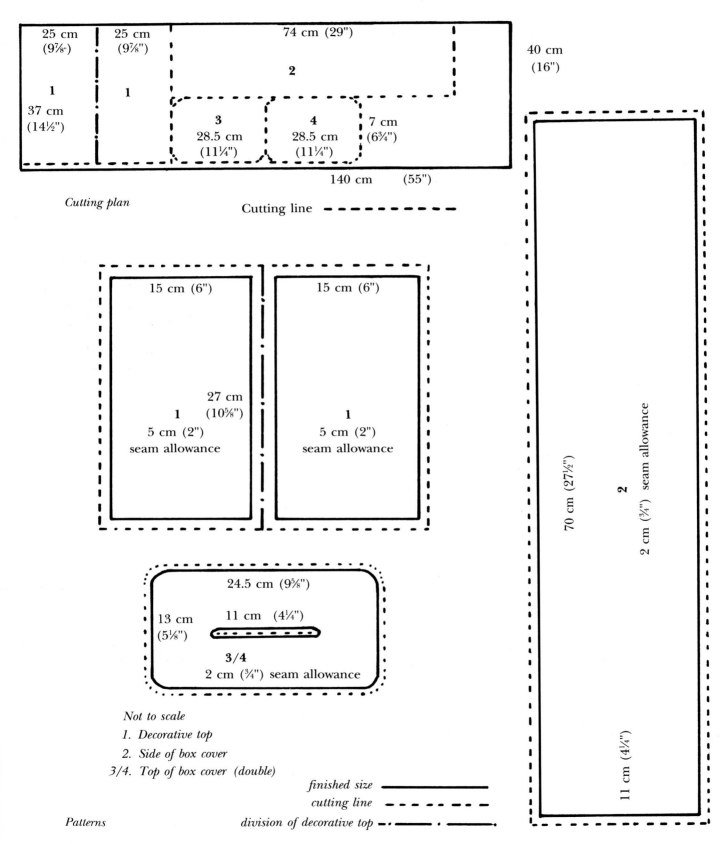

25 cm (9⅞")  25 cm (9⅞")  74 cm (29")

40 cm (16")

**1**  **1**  **2**

37 cm (14½")

**3** 28.5 cm (11¼")  **4** 28.5 cm (11¼")  7 cm (6¾")

140 cm (55")

*Cutting plan*

Cutting line  — — — — —

15 cm (6")  15 cm (6")

27 cm (10⅝")

**1** 5 cm (2") seam allowance

**1** 5 cm (2") seam allowance

70 cm (27½")

**2**

2 cm (¾") seam allowance

24.5 cm (9⅝")

13 cm (5⅛")  11 cm (4¼")

**3/4** 2 cm (¾") seam allowance

11 cm (4¼")

*Not to scale*

1. *Decorative top*
2. *Side of box cover*
3/4. *Top of box cover (double)*

finished size  ——————

cutting line  — — — — —

*Patterns*  division of decorative top  —·—·—·—

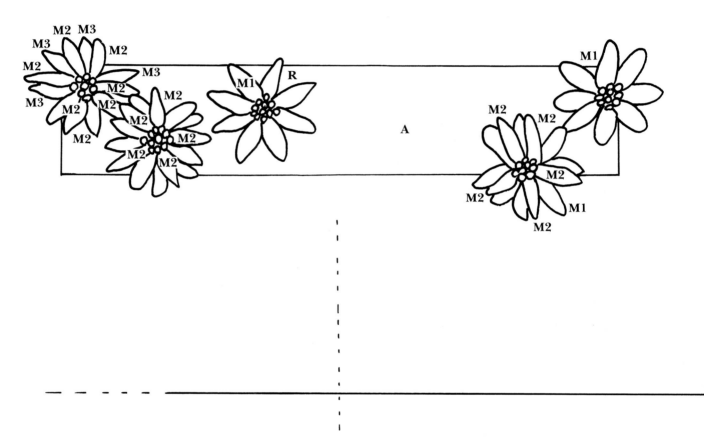

then complete the stitching of the long edge.

Turn a hem approximately 1 cm (⅜") wide around the base of the side of the box cover (pattern piece 2) and machine stitch, leaving a gap between the beginning and end of the stitching through which a length of elastic is threaded and the ends joined together.

| Key | Stitch | Page | Thread | Details |
|-----|--------|------|--------|---------|
| A | mod. 4-sided | 30 | perle 8/3041 | |
| M1 | woven picot | 42 | perle 5/792 | |
| M2 | woven picot | 42 | perle 8/340 | |
| M3 | woven picot | 42 | perle 8/341 | |
| R | French knots | | 6 strands/310 | |
| R | French knots | | 6 strands/437 | |

# Hydrangeas nightdress sachet or jewellery purse

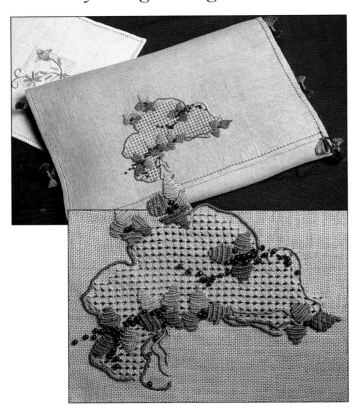

This envelope-bag nightdress sachet or jewellery purse, in true Casalguidi style, is made from one long rectangle of fabric folded in three. Button tassels and buttonholed loops are stitched along two sides to hold it together.

*Materials*
50 cm × 80 cm (16" × 28") Dublin fabric 774 blue violet
DMC coton perle no. 8, 1 ball each:
    208 lavender very dark
    209 lavender dark
    333 blue violet very dark
    340 blue violet medium
    341 blue violet light
    552 violet medium
    553 violet
    554 violet light
medium size dress beads, mixture of iridiscent violets and blue-greens
sewing cotton
tapestry needle size 24
beading needle or size 10 sharps
beeswax

*Finished size*
Rectangle 64 cm × 32.5 cm (25¼" × 13") folds into three to create an envelope approximately 32.5 cm × 23 cm (13" × 9")

## Instructions
Tack-mark the pattern to the fabric with sewing cotton, allowing 8 cm (3") all around for hems and handling.

Transfer the irregular background shape of the flower head and work this area first.

Transfer the shapes of the surface stitches and work them following the key.

## Special instructions
Petals (G1–G8) are worked in parallel rows of single buttonholed bars, using the colours indicated in the key. One colour only is used for each petal. Start at the top of the petal, placing each new stitch immediately under, or starting in, the previous stitch so that there are no spaces showing between the bars.

Beads are attached one at a time with a beading needle or size 10 sharps using matching sewing cotton which has been pulled through beeswax to strengthen it. Take two stitches through each bead so that it sits with the holes at the side.

## Making up and finishing
Make rolled hems (see page 45) on all four sides of the fabric and hem stitch with coton perle no. 8 colour 341. Attach corner tassels made from coton perle no. 8 colour 208 to the corners closest to the embroidery (see page 54).

Attach 3 bead pendants to each tassel, using 6, 7 and 10 beads. To make a pendant pick up the required number of beads on the needle and sewing cotton and return it back up the holes, missing the last bead. Take a few stitches into the fabric to secure each pendant, and start and finish off in the hem.

Make 6 button tassels and loops from coton perle no. 8 colour 333 (see page 52) and attach 3 to each side of the purse, as shown in the picture. Make a shank approximately 12 mm (½") long between the button tassel and the edge of the bag to allow the tassel to fit through the loop.

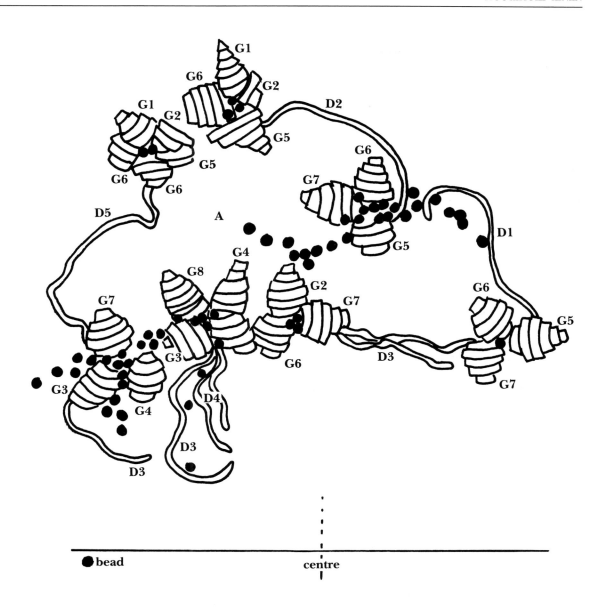

● **bead**                                        **centre**

| Key | Stitch | Page | Thread | Details |
|-----|--------|------|--------|---------|
| A | mod. 4-sided | 30 | perle 8/340 | |
| D1 | | | perle 8/554 | |
| D2 | | | perle 8/208 | |
| D3 | wrapping | 42 | perle 8/333 | Core: 4 threads |
| D4 | | | perle 8/340 | |
| D5 | | | perle 8/552 | |
| G1 | | | perle 8/554 | |
| G2 | | | perle 8/209 | |
| G3 | | | perle 8/333 | |
| G4 | single buttonhole bars | 33 | perle 8/340 | |
| G5 | | | perle 8/552 | |
| G6 | | | perle 8/553 | |
| G7 | | | perle 8/208 | |
| G8 | | | perle 8/341 | |

# 5 SCENTED SACHETS AND PILLOWS

Young girls learnt their first embroidery stitches from their mother or grandmother and then attended special schools, colleges or convents to learn more specialised embroidery.

# Jasmine and rosebuds

## Materials
30 cm (12") square Dublin fabric colour 101 antique white (front)

30 cm (12") square Belfast fabric colour 484 cameo rose (back)

DMC coton perle no. 12, 1 ball each:
676 old gold light
503 blue green medium

DMC coton perle no. 8, 1 ball each:
739 light tan ultra very light
950 sportsman's flesh
758 terracotta very light
356 terracotta medium
tapestry needle size 24

milliner's needle size 1 or crewel needle size 3

*Finished size* 21 cm (8") square

## Instructions
This simple circular design is worked without a background of four-sided stitch.

Transfer the shapes of the surface stitches to the antique white fabric and work them following the key.

## Special instructions
The jasmine flowers are all worked in the same colours, coton perle no. 8 colour 739 for the petals (M1) and coton perle no. 8 colour 950 for the centres (G).

103

**Making up and finishing**

Finish the edges of both front and back pieces with a rolled hem (see page 45).

Join the front and back on three sides with Italian insertion stitch (see page 49).

Make 3 button tassels, each 3 cm (1¼") finished width (see page 52) and attach them to the free edge of the back piece with a shank approximately 12 mm (½") long. Make three buttonhole stitch loops on the front opening 1.5 cm (⅝") wide, large enough for the button tassels to fit through.

Make two single-knotted tassels in colours 503 blue green medium, ecru and 758 terracotta very light, and attach them to the bottom (see page 53 for instructions).

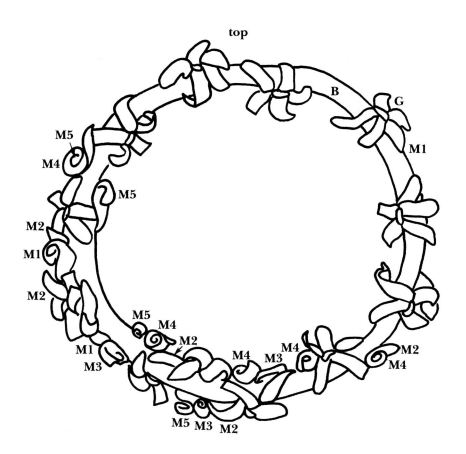

| Key | Stitch | Page | Thread | Details |
|-----|--------|------|--------|---------|
| B | padded raised stem | 30 | perle 12/676 | |
| G | single buttonhole bars | 33 | perle 8/950 | |
| M1 | | | perle 8/739 | |
| M2 | | | perle 12/503 | |
| M3 | } woven picot | 42 | perle 8/950 | |
| M4 | | | perle 8/758 | |
| M5 | | | perle 8/356 | |

# Lily of the valley bag

*Materials*

50 cm × 20 cm (20" × 8") Belfast fabric colour
    641 dark teal green
DMC coton perle no. 8, 1 ball each:
    ecru
    739 tan ultra very light
    988 forest green medium
    926 grey green medium
DMC stranded cotton, 1 skein each:
    924 grey green very dark
    471 avocado green very light
DMC stranded cotton, 2 skeins:
    924 grey green very dark
Minnamurra coton perle no. 8, 1 skein:
    8250 green/grey
tapestry needle size 24

*Finished size* This makes a rectangle 40 cm × 10.5 cm (16" × 4⅛") which folds in half to make a bag approximately 20 cm (8") long.

## Instructions

Tack-mark the shape of the bag onto the fabric allowing 4 cm (1½") all around for hems.

Transfer the rectangular background shape to the centre lengthwise and work this area first.

Transfer the shapes of the surface stitches and work them following the key.

**Making up and finishing**

Finish the edges of the fabric with a rolled hem (see page 45). Make 8 pairs of loops at each end of the fabric strip, approximately 2.5 cm (1") apart, from single buttonhole stitch bars, using 3 strands colour 924, positioning them about 6 cm (2½") in from the ends of the fabric.

Join the sides with Italian insertion stitch in colour 926, starting at the top of the bag and stitching down to the base (see page 49).

To create a flat base (or boxed corners), turn the bag inside out and stitch across the two bottom corners as indicated on the diagram and by the dotted lines on the pattern.

Turn the bag right side out again and thread a twisted cord around it twice, through the buttonholed loops.

Make the twisted cord from four 2 m (2 yd) lengths of stranded cotton 924 grey green very dark. The knotted end of the cord is finished with a basic tassel (see page 51). For the other end, make a bobble from a small painted wooden bead covered with buttonhole stitch using 3 strands of stranded cotton 924 grey green very dark. Stitch four knotted loops in 926 grey green medium to the bottom of the bobble.

*See next page for pattern and key to stitches.*

*Creating a flat base (or boxed corners)*

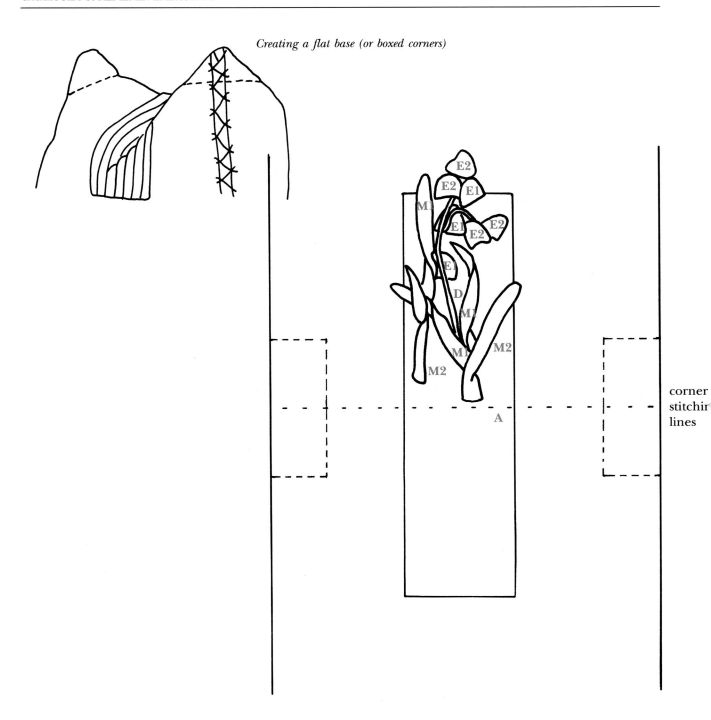

corner
stitching
lines

| Key | Stitch | Page | Thread | Details |
|-----|--------|------|--------|---------|
| A | mod. 4-sided | 30 | 2 strands/924 | |
| D | wrapping | 42 | 6 strands/471 | Core: 6 strands |
| E1 | buttonhole stitch triangles | 36 | perle 8/739 | Row 1: 10 stitches |
| E2 | buttonhole stitch triangles | 36 | perle 8/ecru | Row 1: 10 stitches |
| M1 | woven picot long | 42 | perle 8/8250 | |
| M2 | woven picot long | 42 | perle 8/988 | |

# *Violets*

*Materials*

20 cm × 30 cm (8" × 12") Belfast fabric colour
  594 misty blue

DMC coton perle no. 8, 1 ball each:
  932 antique blue light
  931 antique blue medium
  552 violet medium
  553 violet
  554 violet light

DMC stranded cotton, 1 skein: 744 yellow pale
tapestry needle size 24

*Finished size* 15 cm (6") square

## Instructions

The front of the pillow is worked on a 20 cm
(8") square of fabric. The remaining fabric is
used to make a pocket at the back.

  Transfer the background shapes and work
these areas first.

  Transfer the shapes of the surface stitches
and work them following the key.

## Special instructions

The curl stitches (F2) and woven picots (H2)
on the outer edge may be worked before or
after turning the hem. If they are worked after-
wards the hem of the pillow should be pinned
to a piece of spare fabric set up in a hoop to
avoid distortion.

## Making up and finishing

Finish the edges with a rolled hem (see page
45) in 932 antique blue light.

  Make a 10 cm (4") square pocket for the back
from the remaining misty blue linen. Turn the
edges over for 12 mm (½") and press. Slip stitch
this square of fabric to the back of the embroidery with matching thread, working through
the back of the outer square of 4-sided stitch so
the slip stitches do not show at the front. Insert
a scented pillow in the pocket.

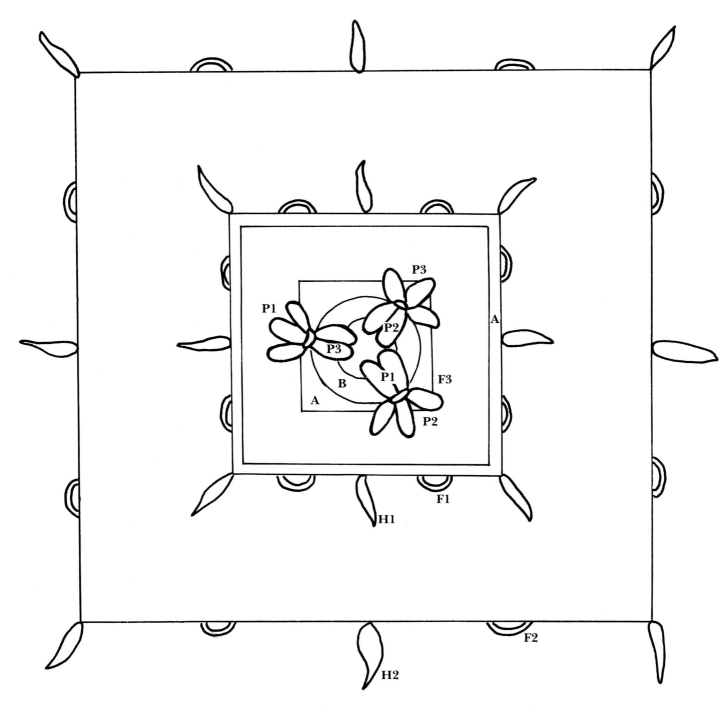

| Key | Stitch | Page | Thread | Details |
|-----|--------|------|--------|---------|
| A | mod. 4-sided | 30 | perle 8/932 | |
| B | padded raised stem | 39 | perle 8/932 | |
| F1 | | | perle 8/931 | 1 strand |
| F2 | } curl | 43 | perle 8/931 | 2 strands |
| F3 | | | 6 strands/744 | |
| P1 | | | perle 8/552 | |
| P2 | } double buttonhole bars/ | 34 | perle 8/553 | |
| | extra row | | | |
| P3 | | | perle 8/554 | |
| H1 | double buttonhole bars | 34 | perle 8/931 | 1 strand |
| H2 | detached as picots | | perle 8/931 | 2 strands |

# *Potpourri cylinder*

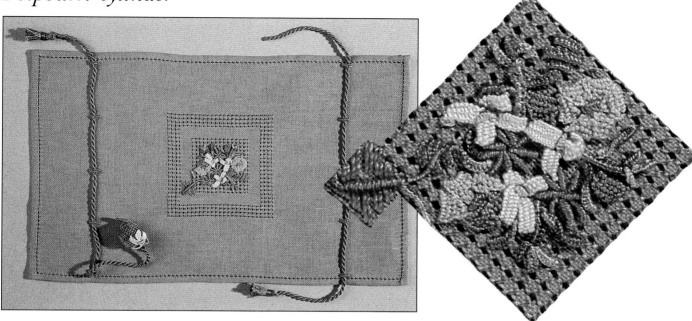

## Materials

40 cm × 28 cm (16" × 11") Quaker fabric colour 610 sage

DMC stranded cotton, 3 skeins:
522 fern green

DMC coton perle no. 8, 1 ball each:
340 blue violet medium
739 tan ultra very light

DMC coton perle no. 8 or no. 12, 1 ball each:
316 antique mauve medium
676 old gold light

Minnamurra no. 8 perle coton, 1 skein:
8220 green/violet

tapestry needle size 24

milliner's needle size 1 or crewel needle size 3

*Finished size* A rectangle 32 cm × 20 cm (12½" × 8") rolled to make a cylinder is joined at the two long edges with Italian insertion stitch to make a cylindrical container approximately 7 cm (2¾") long for potpourri.

## Instructions

Transfer the two square background shapes to the centre of the fabric and work these areas first.

Transfer the shapes of the surface stitches and work them following the key.

Note that the top and base of the design are placed parallel to the long sides of the rectangle.

## Making up and finishing

Finish all edges with a rolled hem (see page 45).

Make 5 loops 12 mm (½") wide with double buttonhole stitch bars, placing them 5 cm (2") in from and at right angles to the two short sides of the rectangle.

Join the two long edges with Italian insertion stitch.

Thread twisted cords through the loops.

Make a bobble with a linen foundation, buttonhole stitched with colour 8220 green/violet, using 2 lengths of thread in the needle together. Decorate the bobble with a flower made of five petals of woven picot in colour 739 tan ultra light with a centre of 2 single buttonhole stitched bars in colour 676 old gold light. Attach 2 chained buttonholed rings in 316 antique mauve medium to the bottom of the bobble (see page 59).

## Twisted cords

Make a twisted cord from four 1 m (1 yd) lengths of stranded cotton 522 fern green. The knotted end is finished with a basic tassel (see page 51).

Make another twisted cord the same length, but before twisting it attach the bobble to the yarn through the loop at the top of the bobble. Position the bobble in the centre of the twisted lengths of yarn as you fold it to twist the cord.

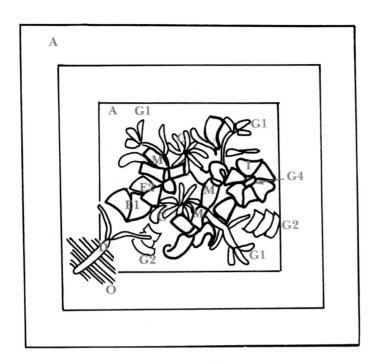

| Key | Stitch | Page | Thread | Details |
|-----|--------|------|--------|---------|
| A | mod. 4-sided | 30 | 2 strands/522 | |
| C | bullion | 38 | perle 8/340 | 12 wraps |
| D | wrapping | 42 | perle 8/8220 | Core: 4 lengths |
| E1 | } buttonhole stitch triangles | 36 | perle 8/676 | Row 1: 10 stitches |
| E2 | | | perle 8/316 | Row 1: 10 stitches |
| G1 | | | perle 8/8220 | Leaves/stems |
| G2 | single buttonhole | | perle 8/340 | |
| G3 | bars | 33 | perle 8/676 | Centre of woven picots |
| G4 | | | perle 8/340 | Centre Venetian rosette |
| I | Venetian rosette | 37 | perle 8/676 | Row 1: 10 stitches |
| M | woven picot | 42 | perle 8/739 | |
| O | straight stitch | | perle 8/340 | |

# *Lavender bag*

This pretty lavender bag trimmed with knotted tassels and tied with satin ribbon bows makes a lovely gift.

*Materials*
27 cm × 16 cm (10¾" × 6¼") Permin linen 065
   colour 38 antique lavender
27 cm × 16 cm (10¾" × 6¼") silk or cotton
   lining fabric in toning colour
DMC stranded cottons, 1 skein each:
   209 dark lavender
   552 violet medium
   553 violet
   524 fern green
   340 blue violet medium
   333 blue violet very dark
   791 cornflower blue very dark
DMC coton perle no. 8, 1 ball each:
   3041 antique violet (background)
   927 grey green light
narrow ribbons, 1 m (1 yd) each:
   grey green
   light violet
   dark violet
tapestry needle size 24
milliner's needle size 1 or crewel needle size 3

*Finished size* 23 cm × 12 cm (9" × 4¾")

**Instructions**
2 cm (¾") fabric has been allowed around the finished size of the bag for seams.

Transfer the rectangular background shape to the centre of the long rectangle, 4 cm (1½") from the base of the bag, and work this area first.

Transfer the shapes of the surface stitches and work them following the key.

**Making up and finishing**
Stitch the two short sides of the rectangle together to form a cylinder and press the seam. Still working on the inside of the bag flatten the cylinder so that the seam is placed at the centre back and pin the base. Stitch and press.

Make 2 tassels from knotted loops in colours 333, 552 and 553 (as shown on page 53), and tie them together with coton perle no. 8 colour 927. Attach them to a rolled fabric bobble (see page 58). Tie a few more knots above the rolled fabric head and attach the tassels to the seam allowance through the corners of the bag.

Fold and press the seam allowance at the top of the bag and attach the lining.

**Lining**
Make a bag from the lining fabric the same size as above folding the seam allowance at the top. Turn the lining inside out and push it into the bag so that the wrong sides of the bag and the lining are together. Pin the top of the lining to the seam allowance of the bag approximately 6 mm (¼") from the top and stitch in place with small slip stitches. It may be necessary to make tiny pleats at the top of the lining to fit the top of the bag.

**Satin ribbons**
Attach satin ribbons at their mid-point to the back of the bag, approximately 9 cm (3") down from the top, and tie in a large bow at the front.

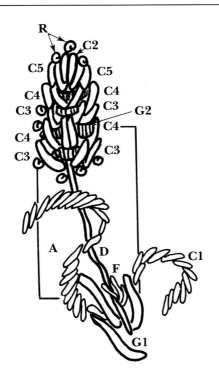

| Key | Stitch | Page | Thread | Details |
|-----|--------|------|--------|---------|
| A | mod. 4-sided | 30 | perle 8/3041 | |
| C1 | | | 6 strands/791 | |
| C2 | | | 6 strands/209 | |
| C3 | } bullion 12 wraps | 38 | 6 strands/333 | |
| C4 | | | 6 strands/552 | |
| C5 | | | 6 strands/553 | |
| D | wrapping | 42 | 6 strands/524 | Core: 12 strands |
| F | curl | 42 | 6 strands/524 | |
| G1 | } single buttonhole | 33 | perle 8/927 | |
| G2 | } bars | | 6 strands/524 | |
| R | French knots | | 6 strands/340 | |

# 6 BROOCHES

Harmony and balance were created by using various motifs based on geometric shapes.

## Cross with green and gold beads

*Materials*

10 cm (4") square Permin linen colour 78 autumn leaf

10 cm (4") square Permin linen colour 24 blue wing

DMC coton perle no. 8, 1 ball: 782 topaz dark

DMC stranded cotton, 1 skein: 3809 turquoise medium

beading needle

beeswax

sewing cotton in mustard and dark green

Mill Hill Glass Treasures 12053 cross

Mill Hill antique glass beads 03028 juniper green

Mill Hill frosted glass beads 62057 khaki

plastic ice-cream lid or heavy card for mounting

small piece thin Pellon quilt wadding

clear adhesive fabric glue

brooch clip

tapestry needle size 24

*Finished size* 5.5 cm (2¼") square

### Instructions

Transfer the background shape and work this area first.

### Special instructions

Attach the cross and beads with waxed sewing cotton, stitching twice through each bead to hold them securely.

Work continuous wrapping over a 12 strand core to form the triangle and stitch it in place over the beading.

### Making up and finishing

Cut a piece of plastic or heavy card 5.5 cm (2¼") square for the top of the brooch and glue Pellon the same size to it. The Pellon forms a padding for the top of the brooch. Zig-zag the edge of the embroidered fabric to prevent fraying and pin it in place on the Pellon. Take the seam allowance over the edges and lace the fabric with sewing cotton across the back of the plastic.

Cut out two pieces of plastic or heavy card 7 cm (2¾") square for the front and back mounts and cover them with the blue linen, glueing the seam allowance to the back with fabric glue.

Glue the embroidered shape to the front mount.

Stitch the brooch clip to the back mount. (First make sure which way the opening of the clip is to point and work out whether the clip sits best at the top or centre of the brooch.)

Glue or stitch the front and back mounts together.

| Key | Stitch | Page | Thread | Details |
|-----|--------|------|--------|---------|
| A | mod. 4-sided | 30 | perle 8/782 | |
| D | wrapping | 42 | 6 strands/3809 | Core: 12 strands |
| k | khaki beads | | | |
| kj | khaki and juniper green beads mixed | | | |

# *Turquoise and violet brooch with frayed edges*

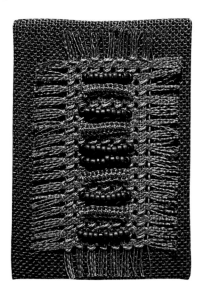

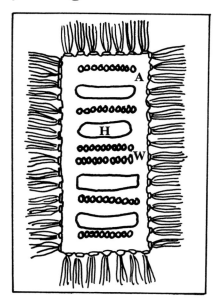

*Materials*

10 cm × 15 cm (4" × 6") Permin linen 065
  colour 24 blue wing (front)
10 cm (4") Permin linen 065 colour 132
  lavender mist (back)
DMC coton perle no. 8: 926 grey green medium
  (background)
Leah coton perle no. 8: 833 blue/green
beading needle
beeswax
sewing cotton, violet
Mill Hill antique glass beads 03026 wild
  blueberry
plastic ice-cream lid or heavy card for mounting
small piece thin Pellon quilt wadding
clear adhesive fabric glue
brooch clip
tapestry needle size 24

*Finished size* 4 cm × 7 cm (1⅜" × 3")

## Instructions

Transfer the rectangular background shape to
the blue linen and work this area first.

Transfer the shapes of the modified buttonhole bars and work them following the key.

Attach the beads with waxed sewing cotton,
stitching twice through each bead to hold it
securely.

## Making up and finishing

Cut the linen to the rectangular shape shown
on the pattern and fray the edges back to the
four-sided stitch. The embroidery can now be
attached to the front mount.

Cut out two pieces of plastic or heavy card
5 cm × 7.8 cm (2" × 3") for the front and back
mounts. Glue the Pellon to the front mount,
trimming the edges to reduce bulk. Cover both
mounts with lavender linen, glueing the seam
allowances to the back with fabric glue. Attach
the embroidered fabric to the front mount by
stitching through embroidery, Pellon and
plastic with a crewel or sharps needle and
matching sewing cotton.

Stitch the brooch clip to the back mount, first
working out which way the opening of the clip
is to point and whether the clip sits best at the
top or centre of the brooch.

Glue or stitch the front and back mounts
together.

| Key | Stitch | Page | Thread | Details |
|---|---|---|---|---|
| A | mod. 4-sided | 30 | perle 8/926 | |
| H | double buttonhole bars | 34 | perle 8/833 | |
| w | wild blueberry beads | | sewing cotton | |

## Heart in turquoise and violet

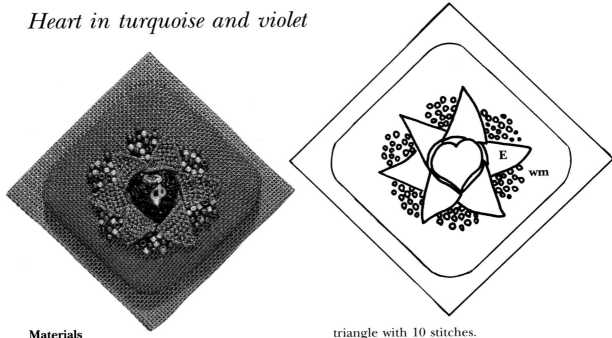

### Materials

10 cm (4") square Permin linen 065 colour 24 blue wing
10 cm (4") square Permin linen 065 colour 132 lavender mist
Leah coton perle no. 8, 1 skein: 831 violet
beading needle
beeswax
sewing cotton, violet
Mill Hill Glass Treasures 12080 heart
Mill Hill antique glass beads 03026 wild blueberry
Mill Hill frosted glass beads 62037 mauve
plastic ice-cream lid or heavy card for mounting
small piece thin Pellon quilt wadding
clear adhesive fabric glue
brooch clip
tapestry needle size 24

*Finished size* Approximately 5 cm (2") square

### Instructions

Stitch the heart-shaped bead to the centre of the lavender fabric. Transfer the triangular shapes to the fabric and work 6 buttonhole stitch triangles around the heart, starting each triangle with 10 stitches.

Attach the beads with waxed sewing cotton, stitching twice through each bead to hold it securely.

### Making up the brooch

Cut a piece of plastic or heavy card 5 cm (2") square for the top of the brooch and glue the Pellon to it, trimming the edges to lessen bulk. Zig-zag the edge of the embroidered fabric to prevent fraying. Pin the embroidered fabric in place on the Pellon, take the seam allowance over the edges and lace with sewing cotton across the back of the plastic.

Cut out two pieces of plastic or heavy card for the front and back mounts and cover them with blue linen, glueing the seam allowances to the back with fabric glue.

Glue the embroidered shape to the front mount.

Stitch the brooch clip to the back mount, first working out which way the opening of the clip is to point and whether the clip sits best at the top or centre of the brooch.

Glue or stitch the front and back mounts together.

| Key | Stitch | Page | Thread | Details |
|-----|--------|------|--------|---------|
| E wm | buttonhole stitch triangles wild blueberry and mauve beads mixed | 36 | perle 8/831 | Row 1: 10 stitches |

# Beaded triangles

*Materials*

10 cm × 15 cm (4" × 6") Belfast linen colour 710 black

10 cm × 15 cm (4" × 6") DMC coton perle no. 8:
312 navy blue light

DMC stranded cotton:
550 violet very dark

Needle Necessities overdyed coton perle no. 8:
883 blue/violet

beading needle

beeswax

sewing cotton, violet

assorted blue, green and violet beads

small piece dark turquoise silk fabric

plastic ice-cream lid or heavy card for mounting

small piece thin Pellon quilt wadding

clear adhesive fabric glue

brooch clip

tapestry needle size 24

*Finished size* 9 cm × 7 cm (3½" × 2¾")

## Instructions

Transfer the design and work the buttonhole stitch triangles following the key. Each triangle commences with 12 stitches.

Attach the beads with waxed sewing cotton, stitching twice through each bead to hold them securely.

## Making up the brooch

Cut one piece of plastic or heavy card the same size as the inner diamond shape in the pattern for the top of the brooch and glue the Pellon to it, trimming the edges to lessen bulk. Zig-zag the edge of the embroidered fabric to prevent fraying. Pin the embroidered fabric in place, take the seam allowance over the edges and lace with sewing cotton across the back of the plastic.

Cut two pieces of plastic or heavy card for the front (the same size as the outer diamond shape on the pattern) and back mounts and cover them with the dark turquoise silk, glueing the seam allowance to the back with fabric glue.

Glue the embroidered shape to the front mount.

Stitch a brooch clip to the back mount, first working out which way the opening of the clip is to point and whether the clip sits best at the top or centre of the brooch.

Glue or stitch the front and back mounts together.

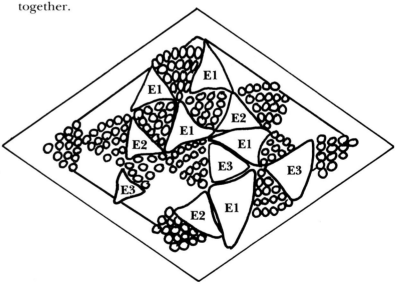

| Key | Stitch | Page | Thread | Details |
|-----|--------|------|--------|---------|
| E1<br>E2<br>E3 | buttonhole stitch triangles | 36 | perle 8/883<br>perle 8/312<br>perle 8/550 | Row 1: 12 stitches |

# CARE OF LINEN EMBROIDERY

## Laundering

Laundry habits have changed dramatically since washing machines became generally available in the middle of this century, when most households still boiled whites in a tub heated with wood fuel or gas. I recall my mother didn't even have a wringer; even though the cotton sheets used in those days were much heavier than the lightweight non-iron polyester cottons of today she hand-wrung all the clothes and hung them out on a rotary hoist to dry. Needless to say, clothes took a lot longer to dry, especially in winter—and housewives had strong wrists! Sheets and clothes were taken off the line, oftentimes not quite dry, folded carefully and ironed, as were the pillowcases. Other times they were removed from the line dry and ironed later; the dry clothes were 'damped', sprinkled with water from a recycled bottle with a purpose-bought top with holes in it and left to stand for five or ten minutes before being ironed, as steam irons didn't exist. Looking after the household laundry took up a large part of the housewife's week, particularly in a large family; washing days, usually Mondays and Wednesdays or Thursdays, were religiously adhered to—or beware a huge backup. Hanging out the washing on the line was also an opportunity for neighbours to chat over the fence, discussing the local happenings, and the pace of life seemed to be much slower. The 'wireless' (radio) was often the only company a wife and mother would have during the day and many chores could be happily worked through while listening to its music, stories and news. No television to hypnotise and distract.

In the 1930s these instructions for laundering embroidered articles were published:

For satisfactory laundering, the following directions should be carefully followed. Whisk a tablespoonful of pure soap into a thick lather in a basin half full of boiling water. Then add cold water until tepid (90°F).

Squeeze the suds through the soiled parts of the garment. *Never rub or twist.* Rinse in cold water and carefully squeeze out excess water. *Do not wring.* Gently stretch the garment to original shape. Hang garment to dry immediately. *Do not use clothes pegs.* When dry, press on wrong side with warm iron. *Never leave garment in wet state in direct sunlight.*

Today DMC recommends the following washing procedure for embroidery:

1. Hand wash each piece gently and separately in warm to cool water using pure or mild soap. Avoid using a detergent with a bluing or bleaching agent.
2. During the washing, if the water becomes coloured, continue to wash with very cold water and rinse thoroughly several times.
3. Roll in a thick towel to remove excess moisture.
4. While still slightly damp, place the stitched side face down onto a towel with a pressing cloth over the back of work. Iron dry, avoiding steam on the embroidery itself.
5. Avoid dry cleaning.

These steps should ensure the best possible finish for your work.

## Pressing

As linen is a natural fibre creasing may occur during use; to retain its crisp appearance it needs to be ironed while damp.

It is very important, when pressing embroidery, to watch the temperature of the iron: if it's too hot it can burn or singe the work. If it's too cool it can crease or dirty the fabric. Use the temperature setting recommended by the manufacturer for the particular fabric.

Always press embroidery on the back with the front face down onto a thick, clean bath towel which has been folded several times.

Immediately before pressing linen embroidery apply a fine, misty spray of water to the back of the work and cover it with a lightweight pressing cloth or a large cotton handkerchief; press

*Household linen—modern pillow sham (page 94) with antique embroidered bedspread and nightdress*

rhythmically and evenly, following the straight thread of the fabric, using the other hand to arrange and adjust the damp fabric before the hot iron dries it completely.

Avoid pulling the fabric out of shape.

## Stiffening and starching

Personal likes and dislikes, and available time, will dictate whether you decide to stiffen or starch your embroidery.

Simple old-fashioned starch is still available in supermarkets. Ironing aids are very popular, although many people feel the result is not always as satisfactory as starching.

Simple starch is dissolved in cold water so that it becomes milky. The wet or dry embroidery is dipped into this, then squeezed well and wrapped in a clean cloth for an hour before being pressed with a hot iron. Dry fabric will absorb more starch than wet fabric so it is wise to experiment following the manufacturer's instructions. Boiled starch is used when a much greater degree of stiffening is required.

An interesting method of starching using rice water is given in the *Anchor Manual of Needlework.* (I have not tested this method):

By placing the fabric in this solution, it will take on a slight stiffness without, however, becoming too rigid. Cook a little rice in water and strain through muslin. Use the water tepid for white fabrics and cold for coloured. Place the work into the solution and squeeze it gently. Wrap in a clean white cloth and press after about an hour. For the inexperienced worker, it is a wise plan to test a piece for consistency and for the heat of the iron.

## Storing embroidery

The best way to store small pieces of embroidery is to lay them flat. Larger pieces should be wrapped around a cylinder covered with acid-free paper; some people also wrap the cylinder in foil first. Always launder soiled embroidery before storing.

For old and special items consult an expert.

If it is necessary to fold larger pieces at least change the fold lines regularly and don't always fold on the same lines.

Regular fresh-airing of embroideries also helps to keep them in good order.

# BIBLIOGRAPHY

*The Anchor Manual of Needlework* Batsford 1958–90

*The Book of Fine Linen* Francoise de Bonneville, Flammarion 1994

*Cut Work Embroidery* Oenone Cave, Dover 1963/82

*White Work Embroidery* Barbara Dawson, Batsford 1987

*Encyclopaedia of Embroidery* Lynnette de Denne (early 20th cent.)

*Greek Threadwork Lace* Tatiana Iouannou-Yannara, Melissa Publishing House, Athens, 1989

*A Guide to Greek Island Embroidery* Pauline Johnstone, Victoria & Albert Museum, London, Crown copyright 1972

*Needle Lace and Needleweaving* Jill Nordfors, Aardvark 1985

Article 'The stitches of Casalguidi and the Art of Embroidery' Paolo Peri, Florence, 1986

*Ruskin Lace and Linen Work* Elizabeth Prickett, Batsford 1985

*Whitework Embroidery* Margaret Swain, Shire Publications, 1982

*The Royal School of Needlework Book for Needlework and Embroidery* Lanto Synge, Wm Collins Sons & Co. Ltd, 1986

*Embroidery, A History* Pamela Warner, Batsford 1991

'The embroidery of Casalguidi was carried out by very experienced female hands; specialist embroiderers who gathered together in their backyards or on the street to work and exchange ideas; in this way their embroidery can be seen as a form of socialising' (Paolo Peri).

Contemporary projects made by participants in some of my workshops and by me are reproduced throughout this book and on the following pages. As in Casalguidi a century ago this work is carried out by very experienced female hands, embroiderers who gather together to work and exchange ideas. Not in their backyards or on the side of the street but in embroiderers' guilds, craft shops and adult education programmes throughout the country, to which they sometimes travel long distances to learn the history and skills of past times and translate them into articles using present day colourful linens and threads, dyes, fabric paint and beads.

In this way modern-day embroiderers' thirst for knowledge and skills is seen as not only joyful and rewarding but also as a form of socialising.

*A beaded and satin-stitched motif is attached to a dyed linen fabric background stitched with gold thread. Trimmed with a beaded fringe, gold twisted cord and bunches of beads. Author.*

PREVIOUS PAGE   *Dyed linen fabric, withdrawn threads, padded raised stem band, fringeing, trimmed with buttonholed plastic rings and decorative knotted insertion. Author.*

*Gold spray-painted tapestry canvas background is embroidered with four-sided stitch and embellished with beaded motifs and tassels. Heather Joynes.*

*Casalguidi bag by Roma Field OAM (1891–1985), worked in the early 1960s on pale blue linen fabric with white linen thread. Reproduced by permission of the Embroiderers' Guild NSW Inc. from* A Lifetime of Embroidery *by Roma Field.*

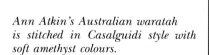

*Ann Atkin's Australian waratah is stitched in Casalguidi style with soft amethyst colours.*

*Jeanette Blunsden's bag incorporates a beaded fringe, random surface stitches, buttonholed rings and corner picots.*

*Dyed linen fabric background is stitched with free-standing petals of buttonhole stitch space filler commenced in the centre of the shape. Buttonholed plastic rings and colourful stitched tassels are made from various threads including rayon cording. Beryl Rutter.*

'Medusa': detail of a triptych based on the myth of the Medusa. Couched gold, padded buttonhole and wrapping. Author.

'Medusa' detail: Free use of withdrawn threads and four-sided stitch, padded buttonhole, wrapping, couched gold on sculptured painted wood.

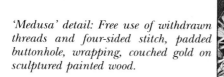

# Suppliers

DMC THREADS AND
ZWEIGART FABRICS are
available at most craft,
fabric and department
stores. For further details
of your nearest stockist
contact:

*Australia*
DMC Needlecraft Pty
   Limited
51–55 Carrington Road
Marrickville NSW 2204
(02) 9559 3088
Fax: (02) 9559 5338

*New Zealand*
Warnaar Trading Co Ltd
PO Box 19567
Christchurch 8003
Freephone 0800 800 DMC

*United States of America*
The DMC Corporation
10 Port Kearny
South Kearny, NJ 07032
201-589-0606
Fax: 201-589-8931

*United Kingdom*
DMC Creative World
Pullman Road
Wigston
Leicestershire LE 18 2DY
116 281 1040
Fax: 116 281 3592

*South Africa*
South African Threads &
   Cottons
Hill House
43 Somerset Road
Capetown 8001
21 419 8040
Fax: 21 419 8047

PERMIN LINEN is distributed
   through the following
   representatives:

*Australia*
Stadia Handcrafts
85 Elizabeth Street
Paddington NSW 2021
(02) 9328 7973
Fax: (02) 9326 1768

*United States of America*
The Wichelt Import Inc.
R.R.1
Stoddard WI 54658 USA
1 608 788 46 00
Fax: 1 608 788 60 40

*United Kingdom*
Michael Whitaker Fabrics
15/16 Midlands Mills
Station Road, Crosshills
Keighley
West Yorkshire BD20 7DT
01535 636903
Fax: 01535 636431

*New Zealand*
Warnaar Trading Co.
PO Box 19567
Christchurch
Freephone 0800 800 DMC

*South Africa*
Mirza Agencies
PO Box 28741
Sunnyside 0132
Republic of South Africa
(012) 669 0125
Fax: (012) 669 0810

Wholesale supplies of THE
   CARON COLLECTION
   (Watercolours,
   Waterlilies, Wildflowers
   & Impressions):

*United States of America*
The Caron Collection
67 Poland Street
Bridgeport CT 06605
203 333 0325
Fax: 203 333 2537

*Australia*
Ireland Needlecraft Pty
   Limited
PO Box 1175
Narre Warren Vic 3805
(03) 9702 3222
Fax: (03) 9702 3255

*United Kingdom*
Macleod Craft Marketing
West Yonderton
Warlock Road
Bridge of Weir
Renfrewshire PA 11 35R
Tel/Fax: 01505 612618

THE CARON COLLECTION,
   LEAH, NEEDLE
   NECESSITIES and
   RAINBOW linen yarns;
   for the address of your
   nearest stockist contact:

*Australia*
Down Under Australia Pty
   Limited
PO Box 9
Seaforth NSW 2092
(02) 9948 5575
Fax: (02) 9948 7172

Retail supplies of IRISH
   LINEN, SILK AND MOHAIR
   YARNS:

*Australia*
Burraweave Yarns
Hoddle Street
Burrawang NSW 2577
(048) 86 4321

MINNAMURRA THREADS are
   available from:

*Australia*
Minnamurra Threads
PO Box 374
Glebe NSW 2037
Mobile: 015 403 137
(Retail mail order, stockist
   and wholesale
   enquiries)

*United States of America*
Julia Golson
490 Forestdale Drive
Atlanta GA 30342
(404) 256 7955
(Wholesale, stockist
   details)

Sweet Child of Mine
139 East Fremont Ave
Sunnyvale CA 94087
(408) 720 8426
(Retail, wholesale and
   stockist details)

*Canada*
Black Magnolia
PO Box 80088
Ottawa Ontario K1S 5N6
(613) 563 4710
(Wholesale, stockist
   details)

MILL HILL BEADS

*Australia*
Stadia Handcrafts
85 Elizabeth Street
Paddington NSW 2021
(02) 9328 7973
Fax: (02) 9326 1768

*New Zealand*
The Stitching Company
PO Box 74-269
Market Road
Auckland 5
Fax: 64-9-520-7575

*United Kingdom*
Framecraft Miniatures
376–376 Summerland
Hockley
Birmingham
West Midlands B19 3QA
021 212 0551
Fax: 021 212 0552

*United States of America*
Gay Bowles Sales, Inc.
PO Box 1060
Janesville, WI 53545
608-754-9466
Fax: 608-754-0665
Internet: http://
   www.millhill.com

# INDEX